COACHED
BY
PAUL THE
APOSTLE

COACHED BY

PAUL THE APOSTLE

Lessons in Transformation

FR. NATHAN CROMLY

 Scepter

Published by Scepter Publishers, Inc.
info@scepterpublishers.org
www.scepterpublishers.org
800-322-8773
New York

Cover design: Studio Red Design
Text design and pagination: Studio Red Design
Interior artwork: Brie Schulze at brieschulze.com

Library of Congress Control Number: 2023949161

ISBN
Paperback: 978-1-59417-523-7
eBook: 978-1-59417-524-4

Printed in the United States of America

Contents

Avo Walthario meo hunc librum dedico.
Requiescat in pace.

Fr. Nathan Cromly serves as President of the Saint John Institute. The Saint John Institute strives to raise up saints to lead by bringing the power of faith to leadership and the power of leadership to faith. Forging a vision for Christian leadership through its unique AUDEO Approach™, the Saint John Institute offers programs across the country for leaders in business, spouses, parents, and leaders in culture through retreats, workshops, classes, and online content, including its podcast *Dare Great Things for Christ*. In addition to inspiring retreats, skill training, and personal leadership development, the Saint John Institute proudly partners with businesses and organizations to provide customized leadership development and cultural transformation. For more information, visit www. saintjohninstitute.org. The Saint John Institute is a non-profit organization.

Introduction

What would your life look like if it were coached by St. Paul?

It is a daring thought, but choosing to be a witness to hope in a fallen world is a daring thing to do. It takes daring to build and believe in a bright world when everyone around you indulges in the carrion comfort of commenting on the dissolution of things that are. It takes daring to tread boldly across the landscapes of our fears in order to follow the pathway of faithful love. Christians are called to be daring people. And daring people ought to be coached by saints who, like St. Paul, dared great things for Christ.

I wrote this book because I am enamored with the hope Jesus brings us. Its secret glimmer in the most desolate places of life catches my eye like a beckoning smile. I am drawn by the thought that the light of the resurrection can never be extinguished and that the Holy Spirit has not yet grown tired of warming our cold world with his bright breast and sacred breath. Plus, I guess I am drawn to the passion and the fury, the fire of thunderous roar, that burned somewhere deep down in the soul of a man like Paul of Tarsus. I'd like to see what would happen if we let him coach us to dare to be saints in our world today. This book is not a work of deep spirituality, and it is not a work of spiritual direction. It is a practical book, written simply to help us answer a question: What would our everyday lives look like if they were coached by St. Paul?

Surely, there are many methods and ideas we can use to shape our lives today. But, if we want to be an instrument in the hand of a God who builds the world anew, a God who breathes an eternal spirit of hope over a bruised world, a God who raises up saints to lead, there is no one better to coach us than St. Paul. Two reasons stand out of this. First, his "coaching" is part of the written word of God—inspired by the Holy Spirit and written down for us as part of the foundational deposit of faith for Christians of all times, throughout the world. This is no small thing! Second, Paul gives us an approach to leadership that is different from that of the world. Its structure and circumstances are the same, but its impact is entirely new. Paul encourages us to engage our world, not for any gain this could bring us, but in order to bring the influence of Jesus Christ to bear upon it. The impact of St. Paul's leadership is not measured as much by the scope of his influence as by its depth. This is because Paul's leadership—the kind of impact every Christian is called to make—is an instrumental one. Paul was serving God—letting his influence serve as a conduit for the power and blessing of God to reach others. His approach is something new in the history of influence: St. Paul shows us that Christians are called to lead the world by following Christ.

In ages past, in times of darkness and confusion, when men grasped swords and pistols to claim platforms of power, God raised up saints to lead. When cultural tides turned, and the roaring of the seas of chaos increased in intensity, God raised up saints to lead. When hope in freedom seemed to shrink before the looming power of the will of tyrants, God raised up saints to lead. The Church of God is not a neutral entity, and she is not the victim of any hostile culture, however tumultuous. Quite the contrary—Jesus Christ instituted his Church to be a mother for humanity, a wellspring of life for a thirsty world and a lighthouse of truth for those who walk in darkness. She enters a broken world to transform it into something beautiful for God. And the Church accomplishes her mission by first transforming the lives of her members. In times of transformation, she transforms her members into saints, and she raises up saints to lead.

The heart of everything Paul teaches can be found in the wisdom of the Cross (see 1 Cor 1:18-21). We live in a time when many in the world are tempted to despair.

Instead of joining the increasing chorus of the world's desperate sighs, the members of the Church of God sing a different hymn—a song of hope: *Stat crux dum volvitur orbis*. It's a Latin expression which, loosely translated, means, "The world spins while the cross stands erect." It is used by the Carthusian order of monks to describe the hope that anchors them in a life of constant prayer and penance even as the world convulses and changes. Indeed, the Cross of Jesus has been the rock upon which the saints of God have stood as the floods of time swept entire epochs away. The Cross of Jesus has been the fire that burned in the hearts of saints who led entire nations through the nights of confused rebuilding. Sometimes, this Latin phrase is followed by an even more poetic expression, one that makes the Cross seem to speak: *Mundo inconcussa supersto*—"I stand unshaken over the world." It is a powerful boast, and it is the confidence of Christians: that the outspread arms of the crucified Christ stretch further to the east and the west than any crazed world can run; that the Cross of Christ has been planted more deeply into the soil of our souls than any defeat could ever reach; that the Cross of Christ rises to heights higher than any anxiety could climb.

It is the same confidence—the confidence of faith in the Cross of Jesus Christ—that allowed St. Paul to bring Jesus to those who did not know him, to plant the

Church in places where she had never been, and to shine a light in the darkest corners of the human soul. Paul, the apostle, could transform the culture of the world because Christ had first transformed the culture of his heart. We see in his life the pattern that God has followed in the lives of all his saints—they transform the landscape of the world around them according to the landscape of the soul within them. God starts from inside the soul—from what is spiritual, beautiful, infinite—to lead the world outside of it. His people are not called to follow a cowering world into craven fear; they are called to dare to lead it into a glorious hope.

Which brings us to the purpose of this book. If we are going to be "Coached by St. Paul," we need to understand where his coaching will lead us. This book intends to help Christians in every state of life find a deeper relationship with Jesus by engaging in the duties of the life to which God has called them. This means that it is primarily for those who need to find a way to engage themselves beyond their fears and weakness in order to succeed at their life's purpose and obey God's will wherever he has put them. When we try to act, we discover our weaknesses—the holes in our lives, if you will. St. Paul will coach us that we do not need to avoid or even overcome these to be successful in God's eyes because God wants to meet us there and sanctify us. Indeed, St. Paul shows us that the "holes" of our lives are where God wants to make us holy!

In St. Paul, God raised up a saint to lead just as he raised up saints to lead in every era of the Church. He is doing this still today. He is calling each of us to join their number. What would your life look like if you dared to answer his call?

Fr. Nathan
Feast of the Conversion of St. Paul
January 25, 2024

One

Freedom's Roadmap

A bright young lad sits in the presence of a bearded sage. He is listening, focused and intense, as he sits in a circle with his peers. A breeze stirs through the Temple, and the smell of burnt offerings hangs thick in the air. But the boy focuses on every word his teacher is saying, absorbing them as sand soaks in water. Nothing is lost from today's lecture, and nothing is wasted. That is because the teaching is coming from the Word of God, the teacher is Gamaliel, and the group of boys learning from him have been sent by their families to learn from him.

With his fellow students, he is listening to lessons on the Law given by God to Moses. As the young boy sits on the cool stones of the portico in Jerusalem in rapt attention, his teacher comes to the central part of his lesson. Looking up from the shadows where he sits, protected from the sun, the wizened Gamaliel closes his eyes and, with a voice like smooth granite, says in a near whisper: "Love the Lord your God with all your heart and with all your soul and with all your strength." The boy closes his eyes to feel the truth with his heart. The others do the same, and a silence spreads through them. The words seem to gently burn inside them, like golden embers catching fire.

These boys are in training, learning from a great teacher about a great truth. One day soon, they will lead their people—God's chosen people—as their fathers did. They will show their people how to keep the love of God strong in their hearts until the coming of the Messiah. Little does anyone suspect what will become of one of these pupils of Gamaliel. Little could anyone possibly guess the intensity of the fire that will rage through the world because of the ember gently catching flame in the heart of one boy sitting there that day named Saul.[1]

For I decided to know nothing among you except Jesus Christ and him crucified. And I was with you in weakness and in much fear and trembling . . .

1 CORINTHIANS 2:2-3

All human beings have something in common: we sleep until we wake up. After that, the hard part begins. It's not that our lives are bad—our days are, in fact, full of many wonderful things—but undoubtedly they are often still a grind. Not only do we have to wake up—a feat often hindered by the fact that we could hardly sleep to begin with—but as soon as we are awake troubles can begin to abound. Once the family is fed and sent off, we find ourselves stumbling out of the door, usually running late and trying not to spill coffee on ourselves as we drive. And, by the time we get to work, we have sat at traffic lights, been tortured by oblivious drivers, and had to stare at someone's

---

1. Inspired by Acts 22:3.

obscene bumper sticker for miles in bumper-to-bumper traffic. And the day has just gotten started!

Yet all of that is not the hardest part. The hardest part comes when we try to really put ourselves into what we do and make a success out of it in the eyes of God. Suddenly, all of our inner imperfections and weaknesses can then come to light. Yes, we have bills we need to pay, debts we need to finance, and enemies lurking beside our paths. The real hard part of life, however, is not the challenges that can come from outside of us. The real hard part is the negativity we can carry around inside us. We doubt the possibility of our future success because of past failures. We worry about the status of our relationships, the status of our economy, and status of our kids' grades at school. And, we do all this with a nagging sense of guilt, a fear that our opinions will be disqualified by invisible powers, along with the residual feeling that we need to lose weight. Sometimes it can swirl around before our mind's eye like a kind of mental sandstorm.

The fact is that most of us carry mountains of negativity inside of us that make the hills that we must climb every day appear insurmountable. And so, we do as most do—we don't. We don't pray. We don't invest in our family's culture. We don't spend time doing what we really want to do. And we certainly don't lose weight!

It's not that we don't have a justification for not living the lives we want to; we all want to move our lives forward. It's just that sometimes we see so much that needs to be done while simultaneously we feel incapable of knowing where to start. How can we be parents when our teenagers won't listen to us? How can we make a profit at work when our employees can't organize themselves? How can we take our spouse on a date when we have not had a real conversation in weeks? How can I look God in the face when I know I am a sinner? Our negativity and fear make clashing and booming sounds inside our mind, and we begin to resemble a small rabbit in the grip of the boa-constrictor of life. It's paralyzing.

St. Paul certainly understood this kind of paralysis. Anyone can read the Acts of the Apostles in the Bible and read about the inner paralysis that kept Paul locked in a way of thinking and acting that he would later regret. Even at a young age, Paul understood the way that politics of his day worked and moved up the ladder of power from being a mere student to being someone to whom the elders entrusted their cloaks as they stoned Stephen, and then to being entrusted with a detail of men to bring a campaign of violence even to foreign cities. He knew how to impress those in command above him, and how to impress command on those below him. Paul knew a lot about power, but little did he know then the power of love that would flow from within him when he would finally meet the Christ. He was used to a power that kept him locked in fear—fear of consequences for failure, fear of rejection by those above him, and fear of going unnoticed. The power that brought that fear enabled Paul to do many things on the outside but it also robbed his heart of its deepest freedom and identity on the inside. When he met Jesus, however, he was touched by a different kind of power—a spiritual power—and one that drew back the strong hand of the fears that were paralyzing his heart.

You see, *paralysis* is just a word we can use to describe those part of our lives where we choose not to act with intention. Paralysis can feel comfortable sometimes, but its consolation comes at a heavy price. The fact is that when it comes to human life, someone is always leading. If, by chance, you are paralyzed in your spirit, you can be sure that someone else will be leading your life for you. Someone is setting the tone for how your children see what is good or bad. Someone is setting the definition of success for your company. Someone is influencing how motivated your spouse is to shape your family's culture. Someone is determining the rights of the poor in our cities. On the great stage of life, the one who speaks the loudest is the one who has claimed the microphone. If you are not the one leading your world, claiming your freedom, then someone else will determine it for you.

You may choose to remain in a comfortable paralysis, but those around you will suffer from the void your paralysis creates—the void left by a father who was never there, by a wife who chose to be unfaithful, of a sinner who refused to be reborn by grace.

The important thing is to realize that paralysis isn't an illness, but a symptom. What the world often forgets is that true leadership is fundamentally a question of the heart. Our English word, "heart," refers to the reality the ancients described with the Latin word, *cor*. It means both the center of a person—the seat of their soul—and the spiritual strength that allows them to move forward in the face of fear. *Cor*, with time, came to be the root of our English word, *courage*. If leadership requires courage, and courage comes from the heart, then the more we can engage our heart in our leadership, the more impactful our leadership will be. Since no one knows the heart better than God, no one leads better than the one who lets God teach them how to lead from the heart.

Like anything that God has made, the human heart has a structure. Knowing that structure is like having a map. With this map, we are suddenly both capable of seeing what is behind our life's paralysis and of finding a path out of inner paralysis and into freedom. From the Greek philosophers to the Doctors of the Church, western civilization has built tremendous edifices of law, culture, wisdom, and holiness by using this map. True and deep human freedom is not without structure; in fact, if we follow it like a map, our spirit can adventure freely upon the inner landscapes of five fundamental challenges it faces every day. Whenever we do something intentionally whether great or small, we engage our freedom. And this means we necessarily pass through five stages. First, we start by wanting to do something. Next, we decide on the best way to do it. Then we choose to begin to do it and discover how to finish what we started. And, finally, we find a way to share with others what we have done so that they can be a part of it. St. Paul—indeed, any impactful leader—has followed this map from paralysis to freedom, and we can too.

You see, Christ calls us to love in whatever state of life we find ourselves—this is our vocation to which we need to respond and the daily challenge we must rise to meet. But love is not only an emotion; it expresses itself by action. And, since every action shapes the world it influences, when Jesus commands us to love as he loved, he is calling his followers into living deeply impactful lives—indeed, into leading their world in his name. Sometimes, this is done by assuming the leadership of our social groups or organizations, but most of the time— and for most people—this is done by making the choice to simply and intentionally focus our efforts to be at the service of God wherever we are. Daring great things for Christ does not always mean daring things that are great in the world's eyes; often enough, we find what is truly great by engaging what appears quite small and mundane. Yet, we need to ask ourselves: Do we know *why* we are doing what we are doing?

This is what being coached by St. Paul is all about— it's all about us discovering and putting the power of our freedom behind the fire of our love. What else is true freedom other than loving truly good things and acting on that love? Is there anything that impacts the world, shapes destinies, and creates culture more deeply than powerful action flowing from true love when that true love is put into true action? Is there any force that can transform the world more effectively than genuine human freedom? If that is true, then imagine for a moment what your life could be like if you lived it freely, bound to the infinite beauty of God by the thick chains of authentic love. Being Christian means shaking off the inner paralysis of negativity and fear, and waking up into loving activity that shapes the world we are called to lead. This is what Jesus is calling us to do. This is what St. Paul did in a marvelous way, and why he is such a powerful coach for us.

We have a tool for making this impact—bringing this leadership—on the world around us in ways both great and small: the structure that God placed in every free heart. It is a kind of roadmap to Christian influence, to allowing our freedom to make its impact in the world around us. In fact, since our freedom is rooted in the deep soil of authentic love for what is truly good, then drawing the map to freedom—the map of leadership—will mean mapping the five stages we pass through every time we do something out of true love.

St. Paul was used to living in a human system of approval where what was right and wrong was determined by the tradition of the human thought around him. The traditions of his culture and the approbation of those in positions of power over him formed a kind of warm womb where he could be assured of the rectitude of his opinions and actions based on his standing with those placed above him. There is certainly nothing wrong with this—it is the way of education, and of preparing young hearts for freedom. Nevertheless, if we are not willing to go beyond it—to venture the wild ride of what happens to our lives when we form and abide by our own convictions—we will never discover the joyful solitude that comes from having an identity that is rooted in a truth that is bigger than the way those who have gone before us have chosen to understand and apply it. Instead, we can find ourselves inextricably confined in the comfortable prison cell of the opinions of those who have reared us—opinions often justified mostly by emotion and denied only at great personal expense.

And so, when St. Paul met the Lord on the road to Damascus, he was changed dramatically—he passed from the warm and cozy thinking of a child into having to assent to truth as a free man. He had to put away the ways of the young and allow the personal love for Christ he had so suddenly discovered to push him into the solitude of the unique identity God had given him—his name. From now on, he would need to find the answers to life's questions for himself. Only he could walk the road of his authentic identity toward which his love was pushing him.

It is the same for us. Just like St. Paul, when we choose to engage our freedom into actions, we find ourselves following the roadmap of the heart through five essential questions:

1. What is the good that I want to pursue?
2. What is the best way for me to obtain it?
3. What are the first steps I need to take?
4. How can I persevere in my pursuit, despite whatever struggles I encounter?
5. What is the best way to share what I am doing with others so that they can be a part of it.

If it sounds simple, it is because it is!

Simple, but not easy. In fact, each of these five questions unleashes our freedom for action, and for each of these five stages of our free action, there are five forms of paralysis caused by choosing to cower and surrender our wills before the shadowy specters of five different kinds of fear. Love propels us forward in five ways. It inspires us to want something, discerns a path to finding it, pushes us to begin our journey, drives us to finish, and opens us to true collaboration with others. Just so, fear can block our path in five ways too. It fills us with negativity, clouds our judgment, and either freezes us into inaction or discourages us from finishing our race, even while keeping us from reaching out to others along our path. Knowing this spiritual roadmap of the heart, and watching for the possible pitfalls it identifies for us, is of great help in allowing us to achieve the freedom of action that will allow Christ to work his grace in our world through us. This is how St. Paul will coach us— through these five stages of action, in the midst of our fears, and into Christ's freedom.

The first kind of paralysis we need to avoid could go by the name of the *Paralysis of Fatalism*. Briefly put, it describes the tendency we can have to not want to dare anything new because we have chosen to believe that no change is possible. Fear of wasting our energy and of appearing to be a failure can lock us into this kind of fatalistic mentality and render us incapable of formulating a desire or wish for anything different or new. Like a rock that always seeks the lowest place, our lives are predictably where the powers around us have placed them. We accept the confines of the status quo and disregard the creative power of God to change things, because we are afraid to fail again where so many have failed before.

At other times, despite our efforts to make plans for success, another form of fear can gain the upper hand and leave us in a kind of mental confusion that could be termed the *Paralysis of Fog*. When we are paralyzed by the Paralysis of Fog we could be surrounded by possible solutions and yet feel incapable of choosing a single one. Like a gas that spreads itself in every direction at once, a person can be afraid of making a decision that would define their course of action—even if it would put them on the pathway to sure success. Instead, they find their path ironically blocked by the sheer multitude of good ways to move forward, because a deeper fear is blocking their path from the inside. Perhaps they are afraid of making the wrong choice and the judgment of others (or even God) when they do; or perhaps they are afraid of some unforeseeable consequence that could arise from their choice and cause chaos in their lives. Whatever the underlying fear might be, it can quickly lead to the Paralysis of Fog and stop our leadership cold. If life were a trip to the grocery store, "fog" would make us circle the aisles for hours only to come back with an empty grocery cart!

A third kind of paralysis can happen once we have made a choice. If we have spent time deliberating on our course of action and made a choice to engage on a pathway forward, we know how we need to act, and what needs to be done. We can find ourselves frozen by a third kind of paralysis. We call it the *Paralysis of Flight* and it refers to our reaction to fear before the unknown, but very real, consequences that could befall us once we act on something. When we pass from thought into action, we entail risk, and we will spend resources we can never get back again. After all, what if we fail? And, what if people do not like what we decided on? How will our lives ever be as good as they are now if we leave our comfortable status quo and change everything by our actions? When we give in to this fear and are paralyzed by the Paralysis of Flight, it's as if we take aim at what needs to be done, agree that we need to do it, and then . . . hit the snooze button on actually doing it!

Yet again, some have no problem at all beginning projects but cannot seem to finish the ones they started. They love the thrill of the quick start but seem to burn out before they can bring their ideas to the finish line. In the presence of challenge, obstacle, and the price of success, the deep freeze of another kind of fear can result in a fourth kind of paralysis that goes by the general term of the *Paralysis of Fatigue.* This paralysis is different from psychological burnout and from simple lack of dedication. The Paralysis of Fatigue settles in and paralyzes our action from within a deeper, more spiritual fear—namely that what we are losing to gain our heart's goal is not worth the sacrifice. We lose sight of where we are going, and begin to put a price on our love. When we allow the Paralysis of Fatigue to take control of our lives, our sacrifices lose their inner, spiritual meaning, our heart ceases its wild pursuits, and our action is stopped in mid-course. Like water, we have lost our energy to drive forward to unexplored frontiers, and we surrender to take the shape of whatever circumstances give shape to our life's trajectory instead.

And then, finally, even if we finally manage to succeed at what we have endeavored, we can find ourselves alone on the victory stand of life. Sometimes the fear of rejection and conflict with others can paralyze us from building the relationships we need in order to build our teams, mend our relationships, and work with the people we most care about. When we surrender to the fear that others will reject, ridicule, or not appreciate us, our actions can be crippled by a paralysis we describe as the *Paralysis of Forlornness.* Instead of suffering from the rejection we so fear, those paralyzed by forlornness create a self-fulfilling prophecy and make themselves aloof, distancing themselves from forming authentic relationships out of the very fear that those relationships will never form. Under the grip of this kind of inner paralysis, we could even find ourselves victorious—successful in our endeavors—yet sadly alone. Alone and forlorn, we can drive people away from effectively collaborating with us and thus hollow out the deeper value from our victories.

This all can start to feel pretty insurmountable. Even reading about these fears can start to make us afraid! Is there a way out of the paralyzing effects these five ways can grip us in our lives? Is there a pathway from the sterility of fear to the radiance of freedom?

Just as surely as these questions swirl around the hearts of all who look honestly at their lives, the life of St. Paul stands like a colossal monument to the power of Christian hope. In the life of St. Paul, we see occasions for every one of these forms of inner paralysis, and through them all, we see God working out his victory and bestowing his influence on the world. Indeed, it is almost as if God does not so much release the leadership of Paul upon the world, as he unleashes the divine power of his awesome influence through the leadership of Paul. Paul's actions in the presence of his real fears show us a pathway around the paralyses that lie around us like pitfalls, and point us to what God wants to do with each one of us—he wants to heal a broken world through us. St. Paul's ability to influence others could have been marred by the same fears that accompany each of us, because we are all sinners. Even so, God called Paul to continually face his fears, his shortcomings, and his lack of strength, so that he could love anyway. When he does so he brings God's powerful influence to bear through his weaknesses as a treasure is borne in an earthen vessel. Paul's life was transformed— not by running *away from his fear* but by *facing his fear*— from being merely a powerful human being into being an instrument of God's leadership for the world. And God wants him to coach us to do the same.

We will have ample time to look at each stage of St. Paul's leadership in the chapters of this book. But, at a glance, let us look at what the life of Paul shows us about leading in freedom as opposed to caving in to the paralysis caused by surrendering to fear. In fact, when we face our fears and let God's grace carry us into action, our lives become the instruments of God's blessing in our world. Our brokenness does not have to result in our paralysis; it can, in fact, become the place out of which a greater gift flows upon the world: God's redeeming mercy. St. Paul's life shows us that the five forms of fear indicated above do not have to end in paralysis. When faced with courage, they can be turned into five unique forms of God's blessing on our world.

Firstly, we can see how much of a real threat pessimism and the weight of negativity was for Paul. At more than one place in Scripture, he recounts his constant awareness and shame about his sinful past—a past he cannot change, with actions he can never undo. The Paralysis of Fatalism was certainly crouching at the door of Paul's heart. Yet, in the presence of his inner fears about the futility of trying to erase his past, Paul allowed Jesus to love him anyway, and as he did so, his heart welled up in new life and intense authentic love. The mercy of Jesus toward him—which he receives in the midst of the truth of his guilt—made his heart abound with a life that overflowed upon the whole world. Surprisingly, facing a hostile world with very little support, St. Paul found a way to glorify Christ in new and creative ways.[2] God blessed the world in a way we could describe as *Christian Creativity*, and the life of St. Paul furnishes us with ample examples of its power to give new life to a weary world

Against the Paralysis of Fog, Paul shows us the blessing we can call *Christian Clarity*. Indeed, there were many times in his life when Paul felt unsure about his next steps. Think of how hard it was for him to come back from his first missionary journey, only to find that Christians from Jerusalem were telling Paul's disciples that they could not

---

2. We will study this in Chapter 4.

be saved unless they were circumcised (see Acts 15:1). Jerusalem was governed by James, and Peter—the first Pope—lived there as well. How could these Christians from Judea come and confuse Paul's disciples in Antioch so profoundly after all Paul had done for the Church? Who was right? Had he misled his followers? Only an ecumenical council of all the apostles could decide the point. In the meantime, Paul would have to face his fear of having preached in vain, and his fear of having misled his own people by choosing to trust totally in the mercy of God. He had to continue to lead, and to lead in the dark. At this moment— as in so many moments of a life lived in leadership—he had no one to teach him how to do what he was doing. And yet, he followed God by the clarity of another light—one that shines in the darkness— giving him a different kind of certainty that we could call Christian Clarity. Step-by-step, day after day, Jesus showed him what he wanted. In the midst of the fog of his mind, God showed the light and taught him a valuable lesson we can learn from as well—sometimes, we only find our path by taking the next step.[3]

Paul also had ample opportunities to give in to the Paralysis of Flight. After all, the hardest part about doing something we love is that we actually have to do it. It

---

3. We will study this in Chapter 5.

was the same for St. Paul. How many times must he have paused before moving forward, wondering at the possible negative consequences that his decisions would have in the lives of those he loved? Surely, many times the sheer fear of what he was doing could have paralyzed him, stopping his forward motion just as surely as fatigue and exhaustion could have set in whenever he stopped to count just how much he had lost for the sake of his love for Jesus. He could have chosen to cave into the Paralysis of Flight as often as he could have quit under the stranglehold of the Paralysis of Fatigue. And yet, despite it all, neither fear held him bound. On the contrary, something else was at work in him: *Christian Courage* shone through his fears as he found his way to his first steps; and *Christian Constancy* kept him from stopping. Despite all that he went through, St. Paul never stopped traveling, preaching, writing, and exhorting. He was a man of action, giving us a real example of Christian Courage as he dared the risks and acted on his love—following through despite the cost.[4]

Finally, St. Paul shows us the blessing that comes from resisting the temptation of the Paralysis of Forlornness. It seems as though St. Paul had no trouble drawing a crowd and creating converts wherever he went, but few

---

4. We will study this in Chapters 6, 7, and 8.

take into account that he had to do it with personality flaws, just like the rest of us. Even though his personality could drive people away just as easily as it brought people to him, St. Paul resisted the temptation to withdraw into the sullen cellar of the Paralysis of Forlornness. How tempting it must have been, for example, to give in to the thought that he was unlovable and feel bitter after he lost the companionship of St. Barnabas! The two had been together for many years, and Paul had relied on him for many things. And yet, after a "sharp contention," the two parted ways for good (Acts 15:39). This could not have been easy for Paul, and still, he persevered, setting off on his second missionary journey on foot across five hundred miles of wilderness. He went to bring the communion of the Catholic Church to Europe—an act that would eventually allow her to spread across the globe. Indeed, in the midst of his solitude and isolation, the power of God blessed the world with what could be called *Christian Communion*. Beyond whatever in us could be the grounds for rejection and division for others, when we surrender to God despite it all, God can use us as his powerful instruments to bring his love and unity to our world.

Following Jesus is a wild ride, because it unleashes for us the power of personal commitment. A life lived in freedom is never boring. Faith awakens the sleeping giant of our heart. We discover who we are—and who we are not—when we finally test ourselves against the demands of true love. We are never more free than when we step out in love toward the Son of God. We have to test our desires against the objective criteria of God's will for our lives, but then we need to dare to try what it seems God has laid out for us. It is a daring thing to walk on water; it is a daring thing to raise people from the dead; it is a daring thing to be transformed. It is a daring thing to follow Jesus as St. Paul did. It is a daring thing to lead. So, how do we go about it? What's the key to overcoming the inner paralyses that keep us from moving forward? St. Paul will show us the way.

Pondering with Paul . . .

Key points

1. Since leadership abhors a vacuum, who is leading in
    my own heart right now? Who is setting the culture for
    my family? In my business? Why are they there and is
    it a good thing?
    A thought from St. Paul: 1 Timothy 6:2-16

2. Every one of my actions flow through five stages:
    desire, choice, action, achievement, and fellowship.
    Giving into the fears that go with each of these cause
    five forms of paralysis: Fatalism, Fog, Flight, Fatigue,
    and Forlornness. Letting God's grace meet you in
    those fears unleashes five forms of blessing: Christian
    Creativity, Christian Clarity, Christian Courage, Christian
    Constancy, and Christian Communion. Which of these
    do I struggle with the most? Why is it such a challenge?
    Read Philippians 2:12-18

3. Paralysis comes from surrendering to fear. God's
    blessing comes when I face them with his grace. What
    is God saying to me?
    Read Romans 8:12-37

Two

With Eyes like
Flames of Fire

The cloaks fell upon his ankles like warm blankets. They came hurtling at him through the air—from the right and left, some hitting him on the back and sliding off again as he bent to hurriedly bundle them together on the ground. Saul was a young man, and he wanted to run with the others as they pressed—a mob of throbbing emotion—toward the peaceful figure who knelt a few hundred yards away. But he couldn't leave the cloaks behind. Instead, he stayed still, his chest swelling with emotion and pride, and stared through the crowd of raised fists and sweat-flecked beards, through the mist of noise and confusion, through the dense fog of anger and fury. He saw the victim's face only for a moment and thought of an angel. The man was looking up, his shoulders sloping peacefully to the ground, his eyes flashing with light, his lips moving in prayer to an unseen God. And then, just as quickly as Saul could see it, the face was lost again behind the moving wall of shoulders, sandals, and hurling stones that blocked it from view. In a few moments, all was over—the closing chapter of the life of Stephen lay written in spilt blood upon the stones of Jerusalem. And, in a few weeks more, an entirely new chapter in the Church's journey would begin as the life of Paul began to roll like thunder across the world.[5]

. . . our God is a consuming fire.

HEBREWS 12:29

---

5. Inspired by Acts 7.

There are many mysteries to our Christian faith—realities too wonderful and grandiose to comprehend. There are many secrets in God that we will never decipher, and many connections between this world and the next that our minds will never make. There are also, however, many truths that stick out to us with stark clarity. One of these is that, when it comes to our lives as human beings on this earth, God is not a big fan of the status quo. Be it in the biological changes that mark the moments of our lives, the challenges that we must meet and overcome as we follow our vocations, or the constant growth of insight about life that we call wisdom, our time on earth is one of constant transformation in the hands of God. God might work in mysterious ways, but when it comes to transforming our lives, one thing is certain: he is always busy working.

It's not surprising, then, that the question for most people is not whether God wants to transform our lives, but rather what we are supposed to do when the transformations happen. At some point in our lives, most people ask, "What is God doing?" Some object to the way that he goes about his work, and still others wish that he would just leave us alone. Confronted by the mysterious and profound workings of God in our souls, we wish that we had some sort of insight into his plan. Why does God want to transform us anyway?

In the Book of Revelation, the apostle John recounts two visions of Jesus that he was granted by the Holy Spirit (see Rv 2:18; 19:12). Both times, when John describes Jesus' eyes, he says that they were "like flames of fire." The thing that makes fire particularly powerful is that it spreads to the one who touches it—as if to say that the consuming love of the fire in the heart of Jesus passes through his gaze, into the heart of the one who gazes back upon him. The author of the Letter to the Hebrews— whom many believe to be St. Paul—describes this truth in simple terms: "[O]ur God is a consuming fire" (Heb 12:29). Meeting Jesus as Paul met him on the road of Damascus meant much more than simply seeing the light of that fire shining brilliantly around him—a light he later said was brighter than the sun that was shining at noon (see Acts 22:6). It meant his own heart was catching fire with the light he saw so that his very life would radiate the light and heat of its influence wherever he went.

Perhaps this is what St. Paul was wrestling with as he lay on his bed, immobile and blind, for three days after his conversion. He had been struck down, literally knocked to the ground, by a light that shone around him with a brightness that surpassed that of the Mediterranean sun at noon. He had heard the voice of Jesus telling him that everything he had thought that he was doing right had actually been tainted to its core by his pride and vanity. He had been handed the heavy yoke of guilt to wear for a past of destroyed lives which he could not repair and damage that he could never undo. He was led to Damascus by the hand of his companions and then promptly abandoned into the dank, dejected solitude of a forgotten bed. In an instant, in the blink of an eye, the thin veneer of human approval under which he had lived for so long was ripped off, and he was shown the raw picture of his disfigured soul. The light was too much for him, and he could not eat or drink for three days, lying in the waste of a life devastated by truth.

It would take something stronger than medicine to heal these wounds. No words of affirmation or companionship could fill the hole that had been ripped in his heart. No human court could come to declare him innocent of wrongdoing. He stood, alone and guilty, before the truth of the Son of God whom he had persecuted in his body, the Church—even unto death. He had only one way out, and it was not through the door of justice; his only way lay in forgiveness and mercy. Only one whom he had come to destroy could put him back together again; only one whom he had hated could make him worthy of love. The only thing that could undo his sin would be one who died under its weight to redeem those held in its snare. He had come to take Christians into prison, and it would take a Christian to set him free.

And a Christian came, one called Ananias. He touched the feverish forehead of the man who had burned with hatred for him. He spoke with love to the one whose mouth had breathed forth hateful threats against him and his friends. He offered prayer; he shattered Paul's darkness; he opened the flood waters of heaven and poured God's grace like a river of heavenly fire over his head in a baptism of water and spirit. And then, he was gone again, leaving Paul only with God's words to him: . . . *You are God's chosen vessel . . . Jesus will show you how much you must suffer for his name . . . .* God had used a Christian to transform a soul from sinner to saint, lighting a fire in Paul's heart that would one day enkindle the whole world. Ananias had chosen love over fear, and had done what only love can do—raised a soul from death to life. Ananias had been sent by Jesus to bring Paul the mercy of God. And now Paul would be sent by Jesus to bring that same mercy to the world.

What was God doing? If we follow the logic of the world, then we overcome strength by strength, and repay damage by returning the pain. In the logic of the world, leadership is the privilege of those who are able to hide their weakness and disguise their disfigurement. As earthly leaders, we run from judgment, diffuse accusations, and stake the achievement of our power on the demonstration of our power to achieve. And here, God was doing just the opposite. In St. Paul, he had made a different kind of leader—one that would shape the world, not according to the mind of man, but according to the heart of God. He had chosen the weak to confound the strong, the foolish to shame the wise, and "things that are not, to bring to nothing things that are" (1 Cor 1:27-28). In the lives of the sinful, the world strives to teach God to obey its logic. In the life of the saints, God's logic saves a disobedient world.

When we look closely at the conversion of St. Paul, we can draw some very powerful practical lessons for the way God works in our own lives. Firstly, Paul's conversion shows us that God usually wants to transform the world outside of us by transforming the world within us. The word *usually* is key here. There are plenty of times when God works miracles. Cars stay on the road when they should have slid into ditches; babies whose lives doctors have declared impossible grow and thrive; storms threatening the welfare of hiking groups are suddenly diverted—the stories abound. Indeed, Jesus seemed to love working miracles while on earth—healing ears cut off by the sword, raising the dead right from the grave before sitting down for a meal with them a short time later, calming stormy seas with a word—but he showed an even greater preference for working the miracle of faith in those who believe. God is not opposed to changing the world directly, and he often does, but he seems to prefer changing it through the lives of the followers whose hearts he has transformed first.

Be it in the life of an evangelist like St. Paul or the loving charity toward the poor shown by St. Vincent de Paul, so many saints of God have dedicated themselves to daring great things for Christ by transforming the culture around them. Saints like St. Catherine Drexel founded schools to educate those left behind by the culture of their times; others, like St. Damien of Molokai worked by every means possible to find ways to treat leprosy. Innumerable Christians through the years have pushed the world around them to make our world more human, striving by every means to permeate the cultures of their day with the liberating truth of a God who loved the world enough to send his Son to save it. God sent his Son to heal a broken world, and his Son sends his followers to continue his mission in every corner of society.

And so it continues. God works to transform the world by transforming the souls of Christians he has asked to lead it in his name. He takes us from sin to salvation, darkness to light, and self-loathing to love. Then, he sends us forth to work the same miracle of grace in the lives of others and the culture of the world. What lies outside the soul—the practical world that surrounds us—is important. Just as it was in the example of the ministry of

St. Paul. God wants to use his followers to heal a broken world, bringing help to those in need in every place and time. Even St. Paul took the time to raise money to relieve the hunger of Christians stricken with famine (see Acts 20:1-5), released an enslaved girl from her bondage to the devil (see Acts 16:18), and healed those who were sick (see Acts 13:11; 14:10; 19:11-12; 20:10-12; 28:5; 28:8). But, the followers of Christ are able to do more than just heal the body. His followers can address an even deeper need: they can bring the transforming power of the loving mercy of God to the souls of those longing for life.

It is not enough, then, for Christians to claim positions of power in our world. Power alone is powerless to do the work that really needs to be done. A weapon is only powerful in the hands of someone who knows how to aim it, and worldly influence is in vain unless it influences the hearts and souls of the people it is called to serve. Worldly power is a fine thing, but it reaches its full potential in the hands of one who is ready to use it to display the might of God.

Secondly, the conversion of St. Paul startles any sense we may have of our unworthiness. Paul certainly demonstrated adequate proof of being unworthy of God's love, and yet, incredibly, God comes to meet Paul when Paul is furthest away from him. As Paul is literally in the act of "breathing threats and murder" (Acts 9:1) against the body of Christ on earth, Jesus Christ came to show him mercy, and as Paul lay in brokenness and pain, Jesus came to show him his strength. This is a constant in the life of St. Paul, and it is the secret to his "coaching." God's strength is made perfect in his weakness. God meets us where we are broken to transform us by his love for us.

In a sense, the only thing we have to lose is our pride. Most of us would like to say that we were able to succeed in our lives without the help of God. Ironically, we want to appear to be like a god while simultaneously denying that there is any need for one! Driven by the lust of competition, pride can make us seek to demonstrate our worth and merit through our self-sufficiency—declaring ourselves the arbiters of our own justification and crowning ourselves king. When we live under the influence of worldly pride, it can be an absolutely terrifying thing to find a large crack or two running down the diamonds of our souls, reaching to their cores. Such fundamental flaws could mean the shattering of a life built on the innocence we decreed for ourselves—a flawed judgment of perfection rendered by a flawed judge. So, instead, we flee failure, seek to avoid punishment, and rationalize away our sins.

St. Paul, however, shows us another way to live. Unable to erase his past or hide the wrongs he did, he asks for forgiveness instead. Unable to declare himself just in the light of truth, he begs God for mercy. Unable to claim any strength of his own, he chooses to lean on a strength greater than himself. Instead of hiding his weaknesses for the sake of claiming leadership, he brings them to Christ to find his leadership there. It is true that Paul was influential as the persecutor of the Church, but his influence then was that of a servant to those in power; only when his sins rendered him powerless did his real influence begin—the influence of a man whom love had made free.

We can learn a third lesson about the way God transforms us by noticing the way God transforms Paul. God does not do anything randomly or without intention, and the same holds true for how he transforms St. Paul and us. When God transforms us, he shapes us into the image of Jesus, his Son. This has major implications for how we understand our lives as Christians. At its core, it means that the goal of our Christian lives cannot be found on this earth. As important as our service to him here is, when we see how God allowed St. Paul to live, it quickly becomes apparent that God has a higher goal in mind for us than any kind of earthly success. More than any human relationships with food, money, or friends, God wants to give us something greater: a loving friendship with himself. In fact, as St. Paul's example coaches us, he wants us to be willing to lose all things—even our ability to serve him outwardly—for the sake of this deeper, inner goal, if it should please him. As valuable as Paul's life appears to have been for the sake of the spread of the Gospel, God did not spare him from things that fly in the face of an earthly definition of success. He was afflicted in almost every way—imprisonment, beatings, betrayals, loneliness, and even bad weather—and yet continued on. In the end, like the world's Savior whose footsteps he followed, Paul ended his earthly life penniless, far from home, alone, imprisoned, and executed by a hostile government. Be it in worldly success or failure, rejection or fame, life or death, Paul was focused on something other than what he could do for Christ in a worldly way. He was focused on something far deeper: he lived to love Jesus in this world and to be with him in the next. The question for us becomes: Will we let St. Paul coach us along the path that God has in mind for us? Do we want to be saints?

What is more, knowing that our lives—and therefore our leadership as Christians—are in union with the life of Christ means that our love is not called to be anonymous. It is the signature, instead, of Jesus upon the world. Our names are known by the same Christ who calls them because they are reflections of his mystery, stars that shine his light on a world that lives by night. We are not called to simply serve the world by acts of justice; we are called to bring the world to Jesus and Jesus to the world. A

Christian leader uses the same tools as every other kind of leader but uses them in a different way. We speak, decide, act, and collaborate, but we do not do these things alone. Christ works through us. Christ leads through us.

It is not always easy to see our "coach," St. Paul, couched in spiritual pain upon his bed in Damascus. And yet, it is here where we can all relate to Paul, and it is here where he does some of his best coaching. He teaches us that the life of a Christian is no longer our own—we have been purchased, and at what a price! Indeed, like St. Paul, the Christian who has found the mercy of God can say, "It is no longer I who live, I, but Christ who lives in me! And the life I live now is a life of faith in the Son of God who died for me." Yes, Jesus died for us. And his death was not in vain. He died to transform us—sinners like St. Paul—into vessels of saving mercy for our world.

Pondering with Paul . . .

Key points

1. God wants to transform the world outside of us by
    transforming the world within us. Where is God trying
    to act in my life? What would God want to change
    about my approach to the world that would make the
    biggest difference?
    A thought from St. Paul: Romans 12:1-2

2. God loved Paul even though he was a sinner. Am I
    letting God love me into holiness, or am I expecting to
    be holy before He could love me?
    Read Romans 5:6-6:23

3. The end goal of God's transformation of our heart is
    unity with Jesus. Is that how I am currently defining
    success? Is my definition of success the same as God's?
    Read Philippians 1:18-30

Three

Hold Your Head High

Saul felt the touch on his forehead. He could not see his face and did not hear the coming of the Christian now sitting next to him, but . . . he could feel him, feel his soul. He felt something he had not felt in a very long time deep within the weight of the hand that was upon his head. There were no words for it, only the sense . . . a realization of an overwhelming presence inside that touch—as if the one beside him knew him somehow. And he did not want to move. Something in the weighty touch of that hand felt like a rich, healing balm spreading over his raw, chapped heart. The man said nothing to him, but a warmth spread through Saul from the hand he had placed on him, and with it, peace. Blind, hungry, and immobilized upon his bed in Damascus, Saul could feel the stranglehold of condemnation loosen from around his heart. He could sense a growing light, somewhere beneath the horizon of his shame. "Brother Saul," the man said, "The Lord Jesus, who appeared to you on the road as you were coming here, has sent me so that you may see again and be filled with the Holy Spirit." The words crashed against the walls of his heart like warriors storming the walls of some ancient city—pressing against the barriers, mounting, and spilling over the limits of his denial. Love breathed fresh oxygen upon the ancient fire that had simmered in his soul, deep within his spirit. His heart quickened, his eyes opened, and he saw the light.[6]

6. Inspired by Acts 9:10-19.

I will all the more gladly boast of my weaknesses . . .

2 CORINTHIANS 12:9

He strides across the stage of history like a great lion of God, this saint, Paul. His achievements are incredible. Conversant in at least three languages, he used his approximately forty years as a disciple of Christ to found over twenty Christian communities, traveling well over ten thousand miles by foot as he summited mountain passes, crossed deserts, slept on highways, and hiked along trails. Along the way, he wrote thirteen of the twenty-seven books of the New Testament, found himself at the starting point of at least five riots, spent over five years in prison, and lived often as a guest in the homes of the wealthy as he was left destitute to survive by the working of his own hands. His presence was considered so volatile to the status quo that at one point he was escorted by no fewer than 470 armed troops to protect him from the forty assassins who lay in wait to kill him, under an oath made to God to neither eat nor drink until they did so. He was a single man, with no money to his name, but the power of his word gave him the reputation of a man who would turn "the world upside down" (Acts 17:6).

His personality was as complex as his achievements were extensive. He was tender enough to convert a widow and her friends from Judaism to Christianity as they prayed by the side of a river, intelligent enough to present the case for the Resurrection of Christ before the leading intellectuals of Athens, and determined enough to spend a day and a night floating in the sea during one of his many travels. St. Paul had the wit to preach Jesus Christ boldly before kings, the presence to confront the corruption of powerful business leaders, and the audacity to withstand mobs of people determined to kill him. Despite the "thorn in his flesh" that kept him constantly aware of his incapacity and inner weakness, he was a man uniquely called, uniquely gifted, and uniquely free.

We find him on thirty-day treks across the backcountry of modern-day Turkey, and on boats sailing to places as far away as modern-day Spain. He led garrisons of soldiers, studied Judaism for years under the tutelage of one of the greatest living scholars of his day, and spent hours teaching simple people about God. He was humble enough to defer to the authority of the apostles of the Church, but he had enough pluck to endure years of imprisonment just to somehow get the opportunity to stand before the emperor of the greatest empire on earth and tell him that he should worship Jesus Christ. The same Paul was deep enough to spend three years alone, praying in the deserts of Arabia, humble enough to receive support and encouragement from Aquila and Priscilla during desperate times, and earnest enough to forge authentic loving friendships with the Christians of the Church in Antioch. He was self-sufficient and so was quite able to live by himself, but all the same seemed to find himself to be the heart and soul of the communities he founded wherever he went. He even made disciples of the soldiers who stood watch over him in Rome! He had the dedication to spend hours, days, and even whole nights, instructing his converts in the Faith, while remaining detached enough to say goodbye and leave them in the hands of others as he pressed on his journey to make other converts. He cast out demons in full public view, was bitten by a poisonous snake and survived, and once even brought a young man from death to life.

Yet, for all of his worldly acclaim and notoriety, he knew how to keep his heart on fire for God. Having taken a vow of chastity, surrendering his body to God on the altar of his love for him, he fasted, prayed, and took oaths of dedication. Whether he was in the grace of mystical elations to the third heaven, in full labor of preaching, or enduring physical tortures at the hand of his oppressors, he lived for Jesus. And, in the end, he died for Jesus—willingly surrendering his life to the executioner's sword. Along the thousands of miles that he traveled, he was scourged, beaten with rods, falsely accused, saw his friends dragged before court for his sake, was misunderstood by his fellow evangelizers, was abandoned by friends, and was even stoned once and left for dead on the desert floor.

In the life of St. Paul, we see the power of a heart that is free. What was his secret? What made him tick? How did he do all that he did, and say all that he said, given the life that he had to live?

There are many places in Scripture where St. Paul opens his heart to us, but perhaps nowhere does he go as deeply into the secret of his inner freedom than what he reveals to us in Second Corinthians 12. There, like a coach, he tells us what lies at the heart of his transformation, and lays it out as a pathway for us, for our transformation as well. He teaches us here, in one condensed place, the secret we will explore throughout this book and allow to transform our lives: how to "hold our heads high" and allow Christ's strength to carry us where our own wills never could.

His words are simple and powerful:

And to keep me from being too elated by the abundance of revelations, a thorn was given me in the flesh, a messenger of Satan, to harass me, to keep me from being too elated. Three times I besought the Lord about this, that it should leave me; but he said to me, "My grace is sufficient for you, for my power is made perfect in weakness." I will all the more gladly boast of my weaknesses, that the power of Christ may rest upon me. For the sake of Christ, then, I am content with weaknesses, insults, hardships, persecutions, and calamities; for when I am weak, then I am strong. (2 Cor 12:7-10)

We all know the story of St. Paul's transformation on the outside. From a law student in Jerusalem, he rises in power to be the one at whose feet the elders laid their cloaks as they stoned St. Stephen to death. And then, brusquely, he unleashes a powerful persecution against the Church of God, arresting Christian men and women and imprisoning them—sometimes, even voting in favor of their death. So great was his zeal against the Church, that he arranged to even persecute followers of Christ in foreign territories, leading a group of soldiers to the distant city of Damascus in search of Christians to imprison. There it was that he met Jesus. In an encounter as impactful as the ground on which he fell, St. Paul heard the voice of Jesus revealing to him just how misguided he had been—he was persecuting the very God he thought that he was serving! After three days, lying in bed with no eyesight, without food or water, God sent a man to offer him mercy. And, in the course of a single day, St. Paul, the persecutor of God's Church, was healed, baptized from his sins, and made a member of the Church he tried to destroy.

This day marked only the outside of the story of Paul's transformation. In fact, his real transformation—

the transformation of his heart—took his whole life. Just as a fire kindles a wooden log first from the outside and progressively works its way within until the whole wooden log has become a glowing coal, so the life of Christ slowly, and yet inexorably, moved through St. Paul, kindling, burning, and transforming him into a true friend of the Lord.

And that is where his life and ours meet. The same God who loved Paul from being a sinner into being a saint loves you and me. The same fire that progressively transformed Paul's youthful ambition and stubborn pride into a martyr's loving dedication burns in the Church's bosom in the form of her Sacraments today. God not only wants to transform St. Paul, he wants to transform us as well. And the secret revealed in Second Corinthians 12 is as real for us today as it was for St. Paul then—God wants to accomplish as much through our weaknesses and deficiencies as he does through our strengths and gifts. You see, for all his accomplishments, virtue, and courage, St. Paul's past stayed with him. It was a heavy burden to carry. He mentions his past sins openly in letters—a sign that he always remembers the guilt he committed—and he tells his conversion story, publicly, on at least three occasions. Who could have hurt as many people as he had hurt and not thought about them, their lives, the damage he had done? What about the children of the families whose parents he had imprisoned—what happened to them? What about the possessions of the simple people who had had their houses looted on account of their arrest? What about the number of people who turned their back on their faith in Jesus because of their fear of Paul? What about the setback his persecution had caused for the conversion of Jerusalem to Christianity? Hadn't the entire Christian community of Jerusalem been dispersed because of him? All of these questions could never be resolved—a heaping burden to be carried by one man with a past. And, if he let them, these questions could easily paralyze him in the passive stranglehold of fear for the rest of his life.

And then, there was the sheer weight of his personality. Like all of us, our strongest traits often are the flipside to our greatest weaknesses. Take traveling, for instance. Paul lists his constant travels as one of the sacrifices he made for Christ (see 2 Cor 11:26). As admirable as it may seem to be able to travel extensively, constantly adjusting to new places and circumstances, it also means that you are always tired and displaced, without being able to take ownership of anything. Take, furthermore, his strength of mind and ability to speak so forcefully about the truth; let's not forget that the same ability that equipped him to stand up to kings and rulers also enabled him to enter into a "sharp contention" with his own mentor, Barnabas, leading the two to part ways forever (Acts 15:39). That same strength also led him to publicly remonstrate—and humiliate—the first pope, St. Peter, and then to write about the incident in a letter! He admits that, in person, his was not an impressive presence—surprisingly—and, on at least one account that we have, he puts his audience to sleep while preaching.

Were there weaknesses in St. Paul? Yes, as there are in all of us. Let's remember that there is a difference between a person having a particular weakness and their choice to act on it. Weaknesses are the result of a fallen nature; actions are the result of choice—and God makes us free to respond to our weaknesses with the courage that leads to holiness instead of the cowardice that leads to sin. You see, our sins are not instruments of God's grace—quite the contrary—but the human weaknesses, imperfections, and inner wounds that can point us to sin, can also, if we are brave enough to be humble, point us to the Savior instead. Rather than letting the flaws in us induce us to sin out of fear, we can bravely face them instead, and rely on the strength and grace of Jesus who comes to save us in our weakness.

The word our English language uses to describe the courage of a Christian is "to boast." St. Paul says, "I will all the more gladly boast of my weaknesses" (2 Cor 12:9). The actual Greek word that St. Paul used is *kauchaomai,* coming from the root word *auxen,* which is the Greek word for "neck." Literally, the word St. Paul was employing connotes "holding your head high" by lifting up your neck, giving you vision and a confident perspective on the situation you are facing.

Admitting our weaknesses and counting the flaws in the diamonds of our souls is only the first half of the story. It's hard to see our weaknesses as the place God will come to meet us, but he does. By the incredible power of his marvelous grace, he transforms our wounds into fountains of blessing for the world, if we let him. It's not that he takes our weaknesses away—St. Paul remained "Saul of Tarsus" his whole life. But Jesus embraces us with our shortcomings the same way he embraced his Cross, and he bids us do the same. Then, he makes a pathway for us to walk. It passes through the valley of the shadow of death (see Ps 23)—the inner suffering and fear that the truth about our weaknesses can cause in us—but Jesus walks it with us, giving us courage. He bids us to not be afraid, to hold our heads high. Through him, with him and in him, we are called to press on through whatever life throws at us, loving him and doing God's will, despite the trepidation and temptation to inner paralysis we can feel when we see our weaknesses.

Of course, prudence has a place to play here, and constant discernment, too. It's not just because we feel that we must do something because God wants us to do it, and sometimes fear and anxiety are God's way of telling us that something is not right for us to do. However, when we are walking on the path of God's will for us, we need to have the courage to "hold our heads high," despite ever-present awareness of our insufficiency. When we do, his strength transforms our weakness—every form of it—into the conduit for his blessing. The seat of our failure can become the throne of his victory.

Jesus walks with us and works through us. How many young mothers have found themselves alone at times, overwhelmed and emotionally paralyzed as they feel completely incapable of confronting the sheer size of the task in front of them? How many business owners have wanted to close their doors and run when confronted by their incapacity to properly manage their employees? How many parents have spent the night awake, wondering how they will ever handle their child's depression? It takes courage to walk with Jesus through the real threats and risks of life. It takes courage to try to act in love when we keenly feel our incapacity to do so.

This is what "holding your head high" is all about. As we detailed in the first chapter, fear is always around the corner—the fear of futility, of decision, of risk, of loss, and of rejection. But, allowing our fear to paralyze us is like surrendering to spiritual death, and Christians just can't do that—our love won't let us quit. That is why we need to let St. Paul coach us with the great secret of his holiness. We need to let him teach us how to hold our heads high in the presence of the weaknesses that could make us prisoners to our fears. Isn't this what Our Lord meant when he commanded us, again and again, to "be not afraid"?

Courage is the key to our success as Christians. Throughout his letters, St. Paul coaches us that if, indeed, we have offered ourselves to the merciful love of Jesus Christ as we are, acknowledging with humility the truth about ourselves and our personal failings, then we have discovered a secret to invincible inner freedom. Trusting in the almighty power of God and his irrevocable love for us, we are able to take a different vantage point regarding our failures, and even our pasts. Indeed, we can "be transformed by the renewal of [our] mind" (Rom 12:2).

By our baptism into the Trinity, we no longer live alone, and our lives are no longer our own. By the miracle of his grace, God dwells in us and we dwell in God. Even our weaknesses belong now to Christ and are carried by him and transformed in the victory of the Cross. Instead of being reasons for our downfall and reasons for the spirits of evil to accuse us before God, our shortcomings and inadequacies—however profound—are now, in truth, the very places where God's mercy can be received by our hearts and from which his love can flow over the world. When we follow his counsel to "lift up our necks" in order to "hold our heads high" when confronted with the truth about what we do or do not have, St. Paul shows us a way to march forward through life. With him, we learn to proclaim a different kind of success—not one coming from our perfections and merits, nor from the support of worldly approbation, but one coming, instead, from his mercy.

When we consider all of the incredible feats for Christ in St. Paul's life, it can take us aback. We can forget that everything he did to spread the Gospel over the world came from within something deeper—an inner, spiritual victory he had to win over himself before he could win the world over for Jesus. The chief battle he had to win, as we all do, was the battle to choose to be humble. St. Paul coaches us to be humble enough to not let our imperfections get in the way of the love Jesus has for us. Following his lead, we learn to be humble enough to boast of our weaknesses, embrace them, and dare great things for Christ anyway.

The more life threw at Paul because of his past sins or because of his present choices, the more we see him turn to rely on Jesus as his only strength and his only love. The more he was made to suffer, the stronger he became. Like an eagle in flight, he soared upwards, spiraling between the two poles of his weaknesses and God's strength. He was transformed progressively by being transformed daily. He walked with all of his weaknesses, yet with his head held high and the eyes of his heart on his Savior. He allowed God to bless the world through his humility. What a contrast this is with a vision of leadership staked out by the values of a secular world! Of course, leading requires tremendous personal strength. Leading in Christ, however, requires something even more: tremendous personal humility. In our humility before the strength of Christ's desire to work through us, we find an even greater power than we could have on our own. This is what it means to become a saint in leadership, and it is the path that God marks out for each of us to walk on as he raises up saints to lead.

Pondering with Paul . . .

Key points

1. St. Paul accomplished many incredible things for God. What is my mission? What do I dare to believe God wants me to accomplish for him on earth?
A thought from St. Paul: Romans 12:3-8

2. Jesus comes to meet us in our weaknesses—where we lack strength. Am I looking for him there or am I choosing to give in to despair and fear?
Read 2 Corinthians 12:1-10

3. Christian Courage is a question of holding our heads high as we face our fears. What am I afraid of now? How can this change if I faced it with faith in God's mercy?
Read 2 Corinthians 1:18-31

Four

In Ashes, Flame

A man in a stained tunic sits alone on an isolated mountaintop that has no name, lost in a sea of brown, crumbling stone. His back is straight, and he keeps his feet tucked neatly under his legs. His eyes are closed, and his face is turned toward the east. A warm breeze caresses his relaxed mouth and strokes his beard, but he does not stir. He is there, but his mind is elsewhere. With an unperturbed pace, his mind's eye soars over thousands of years of the history of his people, remembering. It's easy to do, because the place where he sits is full of memories. Its sands were pressed down by the feet of Abram and Sara as they walked a thousand miles in search of God's promise. Its wadis and washes witnessed the midnight wrestling of Jacob and an angel. And its canyons with their high, red walls still seem to echo the jubilant shouts of David's praise, head of Goliath in hand.

The man sits in a swirling stir of the memories of God's people, and he lets them work their power in his soul, reminding him of the promise and the victory. A pale shade of orange light reaches its long fingers over the horizon and paints his forehead playfully, but he sits still in prayer, pondering. He ponders the weight of the burden on Moses' shoulders as he charged through these same desert sands, feels Isaac's courage stir in his heart as he laid himself down on the pyre of sacrifice, groans with the expectation and dreams of the multitudes who died in the desert, waiting for the dawning of the promise

of God. The man prays; indeed, Saul is deep in
prayer on this mountaintop in the deserts of
Arabia. He sits deep in God. He sits draped in
the light of the dawn.[7]

. . . that I may know [Jesus] and the power of his resurrection,
and may share his sufferings, becoming like him in his death,
that if possible I may attain the resurrection from the dead.

PHILIPPIANS 3:10-11

Every victory begins with a dream, just as every journey
begins with a first step, but where do we go when our
desire has run dry? It is one thing to fight when you have
the energy to do so, and quite another to fight when you
don't. We all know this feeling—the kind of deep lethargy
of heart coming from being overwhelmed, intimidated,
and unsure. The saints knew it, too. In the midst of the
dry ash of what appears to be impossibility, is there any
hope for a flame? Only a fool would dare to dream against
the impasse of what everyone says is impossible. A fool, or
instead, perhaps, someone who has God for their friend.

In our Christian lives, our hope in God is constantly
put to the test. Parents who decide to homeschool their
children because of their desire to rear their children in the
faith must brave the dire predictions that their children's

---

7. Inspired by Gal 1:17.

social skills will be negatively impacted. Mothers must brave the risk of death rather than terminate the lives of their unborn children. Pious souls who lay in hospice centers cling to their faith in the mercy of God as they prepare to meet their Savior. Children who are bullied and pressured to deny their faith in the presence of their peers need to believe that faith is worth it just to find the courage to wake up every morning and go back to school. For all of those who dare to try to live it, the Christian life is a constant trial of hope.

For some of us, the moments when life causes us to dare what appears to be impossible can paralyze us with fear. The cold wind of doubt can swirl in our minds: "Why try when it won't make a difference? I've already tried in the past, and nothing has happened, why should this time be any different?" And sometimes, even worse, we turn against ourselves: "Who am I to dare great things? I know my flaws and my insufficiencies. I should just be humble and let it go. I give up. It's not my fight." And, if we allow those thoughts to stay in us long enough, our frustration can stew into an ugly bout of self-deprecating depression: "The world is no good, and there is no way out of it. I don't see why I try any more, considering my total ineptitude to change anything." Our ability to generate an internal dialogue of defeat can appear to be limitless. It's amazing how creative we can become when

it comes to finding reasons why we should not even try
something hard to do!

With all of this noise swirling in our brains, it's no
wonder why God steps in. When Jesus shared his last meal
with his disciples before entering into his sacred passion,
he gave them a commandment: "Love one another, as I
have loved you" (Jn 13:34).[8] One could have wished that
it was a suggestion, instead of a commandment, for life
would be so much easier! But, then again, maybe we were
not made for a life of ease. Maybe there is something more
satisfying for the human soul than comfort. Maybe God
wants us to brave the challenges of putting real love in
place—even when it seems hopeless. Maybe God wants
to bring us to a place we could never reach on our own.

Each of us is called to fulfill Christ's commandment
to love one another in our own way—it's called our
vocation. Love does not mean just empathy; it also
means concrete action. It means words of encouragement,
hours of listening to sensitive souls, enduring the pain of
generating new ideas in meetings at work, contributing
to conversations instead of letting them dwindle into
irrelevance, doing our homework, and going the extra
mile to decorate our Christmas tree with popcorn and
tinsel, when just buying one could have been enough.

8. Douay-Rheims translation.

God places us on earth for a unique mission in unique circumstances and calls us to fill those circumstances with his love by responding to the needs that each set of circumstances presents to us. Thus, by acts of hope in the face of despair, we become God's instruments in the world—lifting the world up to the good by choosing concrete ways to lead it there. What do we do when the challenge seems beyond our strength?

I remember a time I saw the power of hope in practice. I was hiking with a group of young people up the slope of a very tall mountain in Scotland. There was no trail— we were in the backcountry where trails don't exist. We had to slough our way through the boggy, thick grass for thousands of feet to get to the top. Our guide, a brave young woman named Margi, told us that we would only stop every one thousand feet to rest, and that first one thousand feet seemed to take us forever to reach. When we finally got there, our faces dripping with sweat, our legs hot and achy, the whole group stretched out on the mountain side in exhaustion, breathing deeply. I closed my eyes, wishing that I had chosen to remain back at the campsite instead, and began to imagine how wonderful it would be to ride a waterfall from where I sat back down to my tent below. Judging from the sighs and collective silence of the young people with me, I am sure I was not the only one having second thoughts about our trip.

And then I saw Margi, our leader. She stood amidst our prone bodies, map in hand, looking up to the summit. She was squinting and peering uphill, charting a way forward for us up the mountain slope. While the rest of us were allowing the sheer challenge of the terrain to tear against our desire to climb the mountain, Margi was allowing her desire for the top to drive her to find a way up the impossible slope. While the rest of us were allowing the pain of the process to excuse us from trying, our leader was allowing her desire for our glorious finish to channel the pain required to get us there. She had found a flame in the ashes.

Following Jesus into love is like climbing a steep mountain, pulling against the gravity of our selfishness and the force of comfort into the cold, rarefied air of a mountain summit. We know that in order to love we need to act. And, in order to act, we have to choose and commit to pathways forward through the maze of the concrete circumstances of our daily situation. In order to choose a pathway forward, we must want to reach the goal more than we want to stay where we are. To start moving, we need something that we often are convinced we don't deserve—we need the peculiar flame of a desire called hope.

Nothing will kill the fire of Christian leadership in our hearts more quickly than keeping our hearts buried under the ashes of broken promises, failures, and self-doubt. When we give in to the fears of the challenge, we can become paralyzed into a position we could call the Paralysis of Fatalism. In it, we reason that we cannot fail at actions that we fail to undertake, and so we choose the only logical path to claiming any kind of victory: we surrender to the enemy. Instead of initiating a fight, we allow the winds of pessimism to extinguish the flame of our love and dissolve into apathy.

But Jesus has another way, and his way cuts like a highway across the ash-strewn desert of our quiet despair. Speaking to his disciples' incredulity about the impossibility of their lofty vocations, he said simply: "If you have faith . . . nothing will be impossible to you" (Mt 17:20). Indeed, "For with God nothing will be impossible" (Lk 1:37). To back up his words, he walked on water, raised the dead (three times!), calmed the waves of the sea with a word, cast out legions of demons with a command, and fed thousands of people with a few scraps of bread—twice!

St. Paul, for one, definitely got the message. Deep inside the charred pain of his guilt and shame for his past life, he dared to let Jesus start a new fire of hope for holiness. It was not a flame that came from him anymore— the fire of his dreams had been extinguished the moment that his dreams had been shattered by his own pride. His inner flame was kindled now by Jesus. Jesus breathed the new oxygen of grace over the slumbering coals of Paul's heart, kindling a new flame of hope in him. By God's grace, Paul could dream again, want again, desire again, dare again—but he would have to let Jesus take him there. The ashes of his past would remain; God did not need to remove them from him to start his fire. Instead, Jesus made his flame of a vision for the future rise, even in the midst of the ashes of Paul's incapacity to change his past. Hence, we can truly see in Paul's ashes, Christ's flame.

If we let St. Paul coach us, we can dare to dream too. It may not be easy to know God's will in our lives. Even though listening to our own heart is a crucial step in knowing how to move forward toward the right goals, it is not always easy to hear God's voice clearly inside. Our emotions, our conflicting passions, and the inner workings of our minds can sometimes cloud God's voice inside our wills. So, we can be conflicted sometimes, rightly questioning our motives while desiring to do our best for God. For, even though we need to listen to and follow our hearts, it is not enough to do so blindly. Our desires can be good, but they can also be misguided. And so, in addition to our desires, time, counsel, and patience are needed before choosing the path our desires may indicate. As consternating as it may be, we need to try to align our desires with God's will before we allow our dreams to lead us forward. Spiritual direction, counsel from our religious leaders, retreats, and prayerful research and study are vital tools to help us discern the spirits that can push our hearts one way or another.

This is another place where St. Paul can coach us. Paul surely did dream—Jesus gave him a power to dare great things over and above anything he could have imagined in his youthful ambition. Something happened deep inside the heart of this man as he lay in solitude for three days without eating or drinking, blind and incapacitated after encountering the truth of Christ's love and his own errors. Something incredibly profound was seared in his soul in the howling deserts of Arabia to which he withdrew alone, in solitude, for three years after his baptism. Something altogether mysterious must have been contained in those brief words Our Lord spoke to Ananias when he sent him to baptize Paul: "I will show him how much he must suffer for the sake of my name" (Acts 9:16). Whatever that "something" was—enfolded deep within his relationship with Jesus—it lit a fire of creative energy within him that would drive him forward his whole life.

Just as only the majestic arch of the rocket can fully express the power of its initial thrust, so the best way to guess at the power of Christ's vision in the soul of St. Paul is to watch the trajectory of his beautiful life. He certainly knew what it felt like to press against the cold reality of challenge. When he emerged from the deserts of Arabia and began speaking in Damascus, for example, he met with immediate threats against his life, needing to be lowered out of a window in the city wall to escape men armed with daggers who were looking for him at the city gates. Later, his desire for acceptance and forgiveness by the Christians in Jerusalem was met with the icy rebuff of fear and resentment. And his first successes in preaching earned him nothing more than a ticket on a boat trip away from Jerusalem back to his home in Tarsus!

His short time as an evangelist for Christ did not start out easy, and things did not get better after that. In fact, St. Paul walked a continual uphill path through life, marked with hundreds of opportunities to give in and stop trying. From the sheer physicality of walking across what is modern-day Turkey for Jesus, to the need to justify some of the decisions he made in his work as an evangelizer amidst "much debate" at the Council of Jerusalem (see Acts 15:7); from being publicly thrashed with rods and dragged through the main square of the city of Philippi without a trial and without consideration of his Roman citizenship, to having to flee over fifty miles at night to escape a jealous mob in Thessalonica, St. Paul had hundreds of reasons to stop pursuing his mission. But he had one reason to keep going: his love for Jesus.

And that one reason was all that he needed. With head "held high," St. Paul boasted of those reasons to fear the futility of his efforts. He braved the apparent frustration of his dreams, and "urged on" by the love of Christ, he pivoted, expanded his vision, and innovated. Obstacles rarely had the final word for St. Paul—instead, he took circumstances as God's sealed orders, and, as a river allows its banks to channel its energy into a beautiful flow, he allowed frustrations and an apparently hostile status quo to direct his course to the new things that God wanted to do through him. This is the hallmark of what we call Christian Creativity—God works out new and better solutions in and through situations of apparent frustration and impossibility.

For example, being rejected by the community in Jerusalem opened Paul to receiving love and encouragement from the fervent Church in Antioch, forming friendships there that he kept for his whole life. Meeting with the refusal of the Jewish community to allow him to preach in their synagogues became an opportunity for him to reach out to the gentiles. Even being locked in prison three times became an opportunity for something new—he converted and baptized his jailer in Philippi, preached to the ruler of Israel while in prison in Jaffa, and began to convert a cohort of centurions under house arrest in Rome. His lack of money allowed him to convert his future employers,

Priscilla and Aquila, and make saints out of them. Driven by riotous mobs from Thessalonica and Berea, he found himself with the opportunity to stand before the greatest minds of Athens at the Areopagus. Throughout his life, St. Paul allowed God to mold and shape him, like clay in the hands of a master potter, both through the trials and stumbling blocks on his path, as well as by God's constant inspiration to keep moving forward. And that is where St. Paul becomes such a great coach for us. Most of us would never dream of doing things on a similar scale. When we read his life, we can even feel small and inadequate. We have to remember that, of course, Paul was an incredibly driven person. But the inspired legacy that he left behind did not come from his drive alone—just as the impact of our lives is not merely a function of the unique set of gifts God gave us. Rather, Paul's inner fire came like a flame from God in the midst of the ashes of the broken circumstances that surrounded his life. The same is true for us in our own limitations and constraints.

In contrast with the worldly vision of leadership so prevalent today, Paul's humility coaches us not to glorify ourselves. He did not merely choose to imprint his likeness upon the world; he chose to leave behind the face of Christ instead. This is what is different about Christian leadership—the difference we make comes from and belongs to Christ. As members of his body, we do all that we do as his instruments—allowing God to grace the world through our humble efforts. And God can use the humble, the weak, and the broken just as well as he can use the gifted and driven.

For all of his natural gifts and abilities, St. Paul is an example of someone who let God use his weakness as much as he let God use his gifts. He held his head high amid the refusals he was served, and waited there for what God would do next. He chose to trust in God in the midst of the ambient cultural sloth embraced by those in his day who yearned for nothing new, and peacefully continued to assert his confident hope that God had a desire to renew the world. He was humbled in the eyes of the world—appearing defeated, crushed down, and abandoned in the eyes of those who saw him. Yet, his apparent defeats, endured with courage, allowed the love of Christ to do something entirely new, blessing the world with Christian Creativity. St. Paul teaches us to look for the flame in the midst of the ashes because God is the master of the fire, and God always finds a way. God's way did not always look as St. Paul could have envisioned. But, letting go of what is in the past, and straining forward to lay hold of the one who had laid hold of him, St. Paul dared the impossible and found God's will on the other side.

So, what if we let St. Paul coach us here? What can we learn from him? At the root of his ability to transform what could be negative circumstances into positive results is the way he chooses to look at things. Foundationally, he allowed his faith in the creative power of God's love to be the lens through which he looked at the world. We can do the same. The truth that God reveals to us is always fundamentally positive and points us toward our fulfillment—even if hard things or profound suffering might be a part of our path. God is good. God loves us. And God is in control . . . of everything. God knows the future as well as the past, and God's love will work everything out for the good for those who love him. St. Paul chose to believe this. He chose faith over fear. He chose to believe in the dawn, even when he was sitting in the dark of night. And, in the light of that faith, he found a path forward. What would our lives look like if we chose to light the candle of faith in the gloom that surrounds us instead of cursing the ambient darkness?

Other saints have done the same. Saints like Francis Xavier Cabrini faced her fear of drowning and, in the light of God's providence, crossed the ocean on a boat twenty-seven times as she went about founding over forty hospitals, orphanages, and schools for the poor. Mother Teresa of Calcutta was able to look past the "distressing disguise" of the most desperate and harsh sides of poverty to find the face of Jesus there. St. John Bosco and the order he founded transformed the lives of thousands of boys whom the world had destined for life in gangs on the street into men of virtue and family. The Christian faith gives us the ability even to peer into a tomb with the hope that we will find evidence of the resurrection there, because we walk as if seeing the invisible. If we choose to renew our minds by faith, we can walk in the hopeful light of faith in a gracious God.

In many ways, our world is a lot like the world of St. Paul. As our culture establishes norms and customs without reference to God and his inspired Word, the Bible, Christians are increasingly faced with ways of life that appear to make their witness ineffective. The stronger a secularized culture becomes, the harder it will become for Christians to maintain their hope in the vision that Christ lays out for their families, their businesses, and their culture. Just like the Christians in the days of St. Paul, we can be tempted to believe that the power of the Resurrection has been exhausted, and that the Church's candle will be snuffed out by the strong winds that blow against her. And yet, just like St. Paul, there are those who choose the darkest hours of the night to begin their watch for the dawn. The power to dream—to hope for what is not visible or even known—is a gift God put in St. Paul's heart even as he forged a path in the wilderness of his life's journey. It is a flame that can burn in our hearts too—the light and heat of the Resurrection burning in the midst of the cold ash of a world that has forgotten how to hope.

Pondering with Paul . . .

Key points

1. The fear that our actions will be fruitless can make
    our lives meaningless. Do I feel trapped by the
    circumstances of my life? Do I believe that any of them
    are stronger than God?
    A thought from St. Paul: Acts 16:16-39

2. God is always ready to do new things in our lives. Are
    we clinging to our past? What do we need to let go of
    to let him do something new?
    Read 2 Corinthians 5:17-21

3. St. Paul hoped in the goodness of God, and that hope
    opened the door for God to lead him in goodness
    and grace. What can I do to keep the flame of hope
    burning strong in my life?
    Read 1 Corinthians 15:50-58

Five

In Darkness, Light

It was not supposed to happen this way. He could feel the hot sands against his cheek, and his bruised shoulder stabbed him with pain as his body pressed its full weight upon the ground. Heavy stones smacked against his arms, thudded into the flesh of his stomach, and cracked against his skull. He writhed like an animal, flailing his arms, shielding his head. He could hear the voices of the men around him but could no longer see anything and could only taste his own blood in his mouth. He did not have much more time. He could not resist much longer. His mind raced to his friends whom he had brought into this mess, to Barnabas, to Lois, to young Timothy. What would happen to them? How would they escape? What had he done? Where would they go? But the ugly face of sheer pain flashed through his terrifying thoughts. He could no longer see. He could hardly breathe. He could only feel pain. Paul had begun his life as a missionary with bold strength. He was now ending it, a few short months after it had begun, in absolute defeat. There was no way out, and no way forward for his mission. Instead, he entered into utter darkness, stoned by a crowd of furious men and left for dead upon the desert sands of Lystra.[9]

We are treated as impostors, and yet are true; as unknown, and yet well known; as dying, and behold we live . . .

2 CORINTHIANS 6:8-9

9. Inspired by Acts 14:19-28.

In my work as a priest training Christians to lead, I like to begin my workshops by asking what inner obstacle my audience is struggling with the most. I have come to learn that the particular obstacles we face on the outside are never the real problem. Having problems is not the problem. Having problems with having problems—that's the real problem! Those struggling with various leadership issues all have something in common—they are paralyzed to some degree into inaction by refusing to face a shadow of fear they sensed inside them: fear of futility, fear of being wrong, fear of risk, fear of loss, or fear of rejection. In my survey over the years of Christians who are called to lead, the most common reason for paralysis by far is the fear of making the wrong decision. In our ministry, we call it the Paralysis of Fog.

The Paralysis of Fog, as we define it in our work, is more than not knowing what to decide—it is a phenomenon that occurs because we are *unable* to decide. How many great ideas never come to the light of day because they were never tried! How many solutions to our problems lay unactuated and crumpled up on the table of our dreams because we could not find our way to put them into practice! Having the fire of love push us to want to try to do something daring is a beautiful first step to leadership, but it is not enough. Love requires vision to become effective action. Loving desire is necessary for every great action, but so are the choices and decisions about how to make that love real. Love warms the heart and mind, but, as the saying goes, "You can't eat love!" Something more is needed. We have to choose the right pathway forward among many possible routes. And this is where many stumble.

To lead others effectively, we have to pass over from the warm, soft shores of our dreams onto the cold, hardened land of action by the singular bridge of making decisions about how we will get there. Our love points us toward the goal we desire to obtain, but more is needed if we are to lead—we have to decide *how* we are going to accomplish our goals.

It is hard to do—especially when we want to do what is right. How do we know the right way to care for our aging parents? How many children ought we to have in our family? How do we know that the person we love is the right one to marry? Who is to say whether we go to a relative's wedding when they marry outside of the Church? There are so many questions and, sometimes, it seems like there are very few answers upon which we can rely. There are also so many options—how can we know which is the right way to do what we need to do? This is where the challenge begins.

The task of mapping out a single day can prove exhausting in itself—let alone making major decisions about life and its future. There is no road map to what God wants us to do in our lives, and even when we make a decision there are scores and scores of critics who stand along our path and tell us that the way that we are walking is wrong or will never work. It's no wonder so few people want to claim the ownership and responsibility for which leadership calls. It is so much easier to remain silent and be thought a fool than open our mouths and remove all doubt! The simple fact is that if I simply do what everyone else does, I will always be thought to be right by the crowd. The world often measures success more by the absence of criticism by others than by the criteria of the truth of our destiny as willed by God. And all of these fears can reach up from within our hearts and cloud our minds, paralyzing us by keeping us from being able to make a choice.

At its root, the real problem of this kind of fearful indecision does not come from the multiplicity of possible ideas and ways to express the love that burns in our hearts. The real problem lies inside of us—our fear of not making the best choice. Be it a fear of the harsh judgments of others, or the genuine dread of unanticipated negative consequences from unforeseeable hazards, or many other possible negative eventualities, our ability to chart a course forward amidst the vicissitudes of life can easily become paralyzed by deeper fears about being wrong. Like a thick blanket, our inner light is darkened by the unknown and the unknowable—the chaos of our lives and our inability to control it.

When we allow our fear of making the wrong choice to paralyze us, our lives tend to follow a pattern that will forever keep us in the status quo. We become paralyzed in our actions, because we choose to ignore the warm and wild summons of truth, preferring to listen to the ceaseless clamor of confused opinions instead. We have to learn how to face this fear. St. Paul can coach us here. If we do not face our fear and step forward to make the best decision we can when we must, we will instead surrender our power to choose to those who have chosen to lead us. We will become mere followers—paying for our freedom from the pain of responsibility with the currency of our personal hopes and dreams. The inner paralysis we call the Paralysis of Fog kills the effects of our leadership because it keeps us from naming and claiming the love at the root of our desires. We choose to remain in the dark, inactive and passive, because it is easier than looking for the right path on which to walk.

There were many times in the life of St. Paul when he was in the dark, not knowing which way to go. Even a cursory glance at his life reveals a man who had to make an uncommon number of major decisions without any fixed reference point. He could not rely on the New Testament to guide him—he was writing the New Testament! He could not make a novena to St. Paul—he *was* St. Paul! He could not ask for advice from his community—he was founding the community! Paul had to rely on something else to guide him—a light that shines in the darkness of unknowing, the light of the Holy Spirit.

To St. Paul, the Holy Spirit was a constant companion, and his teachings on the Holy Spirit give light to anyone who wants to let Paul coach them in their walk with Christ. The Holy Spirit literally "filled" Paul the moment he recovered his sight, and then enveloped Paul as he was baptized in his holy Name (see Acts 9:17-18). It was the Holy Spirit who asked the Christians in Antioch to set Paul and Barnabas apart for the work to which he was calling them and then sent them on their first missionary journey (see Acts 13:4). He spoke his word through Paul's words and was made manifest in the Christian community through Paul's presence. Sometimes, the Holy Spirit stopped Paul, forbidding him to speak (see Acts 16:6), and at other times, when Paul laid hands on people, the Holy Spirit caused them to speak in foreign languages (see Acts 19:6). He even spoke directly to Paul on occasions, telling him what to do and what would happen to him (see Acts 20:23; 21:11). Perhaps this is shared with all of us in the Scriptures in order to help us understand how powerful a gift God gave to us when he gave us that same Holy Spirit!

Indeed, the Holy Spirit has been given to us just as he was given to the early Christians—through holy baptism, through the proclamation of the word by Paul and the other apostles, and through the laying on of hands of the apostles. Paul reminds us that the Holy Spirit dwells in Christians (see 1 Cor 3:16; 2 Tm 1:14), repairs the wounds of sin in us (see Ti 3:5), allows us to experience God's power as God wills (see 1 Thes 1:5; Rom 15:13), and gives us gifts for us to share with others (see 1 Cor. 12:1-11). This means we do not need to live as other people live—in fear, in doubt, in despair; instead, with the love of God poured into our hearts by the Holy Spirit, we have a sure hope (see Rom 5:5). By him, we have a unique intimacy with God—knowing his deep "thoughts" and calling him "Abba" like Jesus (see 1 Cor 2:11; Rom 8:15)—and a profound fellowship with one another (see 2 Cor 13:14). What a gift! And he will move us as he moved St. Paul, through the quiet light of his truth, even if it is a light that shines within the cloud of our greater unknowing. His light might not always give us human certainty, but he works in another way, demonstrating what we can call Christian Clarity. Indeed, this Christian Clarity is a unique kind of clarity. The light of the Holy Spirit never gives us the kind of certitude our fearful hearts crave—a certitude that would remove from us the responsibility we so dread and God so desires. When we follow God into impactful living, there will always be room for us to question our actions and decisions if we want to. There will always be room for human error. It's almost as if the Holy Spirit is not afraid of our errors or our poor decisions. If he was, he would make them impossible for us. On the contrary, he seems much more concerned about confronting our fear about making them! He gives us a light that shines in the darkness—a light only visible through the eyes of a trust that dares the unknown future because of the known promise.

Wasn't it St. Paul who wrote those hope-filled words of trust in God's providence: "If God is for us, who is against us?" (Rom 8:31). Trust in God's Providence is exactly what he would need, again and again. Think about what happened to him in Lystra, where his first missionary journey came to a screeching halt as a crowd of angry men threw stones at his head until they thought that he was dead. How was he to know whether going there was the right move for him and his companions? Or think about the sharp contention that he had with St. Barnabas about whether to take John Mark along with them on their second missionary journey. It is never easy to disagree with someone you care about—and even more so when they break off your relationship with them and refuse to go with you, because they thought that you were wrong. How could Paul have known whether or not he was right? Even without knowing with absolute certitude, however, he decided. It was as if he walked by a different kind of light. Perhaps the absolute certainty our fearful hearts crave is not the most important thing. Perhaps, instead, the key to following God's will lies in entrusting ourselves humbly and constantly to the Holy Spirit, allowing God to make all things work out for the good in his perfect time.

St. Paul's decisions sometimes endangered the well-being of his friends and followers—one of them, Jason, even had his livelihood threatened because he had given hospitality to Paul in Thessalonica. His doctrine was questioned at great length by the other apostles in the council of Jerusalem. His preaching won followers who sold what they had and moved with him—like Priscilla and Aquila—making him in part responsible for inspiring them on a path that would take their lives in whole new, unpredictable, directions. Would they blame him when they were forced to sleep on the side of the road? Would they give up when it got hard and leave him stranded? Would they say the wrong thing, chasing away potential converts? Would they betray him and turn him over to his enemies? There was no way for Paul to know any of that. And yet, he still began communities—even without a pre-set structural plan on how to do so. He supplied for the needs of all without any source of income, found his way to destinations without knowing where he was going beforehand, and founded churches where there were none before.

St. Paul was a founder—a leader in every sense of the term. And, founders make a business out of walking in the fog of uncertainties and unforeseeable circumstances. That's what leaders must do—they go first, bringing the light of their vision into places that were bereft of it before they arrived. While that might sound glorious, it is, in fact, a heavy cross. Going where there is no path means walking without a map. Jesus seems to not mind asking his followers to do just that. His footsteps might be invisible, but if we trust him, he will bring us to walk in them by the power of his grace. When we do, when we courageously hold our heads high and "boast" of the obscurity before us, we leave the world a witness of a different kind of leadership—one that allows God to lead the world by shining with clarity within our obscurity. We show the world that there is another light that guides our steps—the invisible brilliance of the light of the Holy Spirit.

But, learning how to follow the light of the Holy Spirit in the dark of uncertainty and questioning does not mean that planning is unnecessary. Quite the contrary! Our Lord taught us to be like a king who counts his troops before attacking a foreign army and like a builder who counts his resources before committing to build (see Lk 14:31). Even though he was God and therefore beyond all strategy and human planning, he revealed to his apostles that he was following the Father's will for his life and making decisions accordingly. He asks us to do our best to be humanly prudent, even while accepting that our prudence might not always give the ultimate answer. A big help in this prudence comes from actually taking the time to question our motives and examine our consciences in the light of the Church's spiritual tradition. Spiritual reading from the saints, spiritual direction from a priest or religious leader, or time away on retreat in prayer, all form part of the priceless tools leaders need to avail themselves of in order to hear the voice of God better amidst the many options that vie for our commitment.

St. Paul took Christ's instruction about the need for prudence to heart as well. He made many intentional decisions, revealing his ability to choose and discern; he tried to plot out the best way to follow his heart's desire to make Christ known. Before striking off on a lifetime of preaching to the gentiles, for example, he made sure to submit his efforts to the approval of the apostles, lest he labor in vain. He chose the efficient means of letter writing to make his teaching better known. He chose to invest in followers who would, in turn, become future leaders. He chose to go to Jerusalem and preach there, even though he was warned explicitly on three separate occasions that preaching there would result in his imprisonment. He chose people in whom to confide carefully, avoiding those who could entrap or betray him. He was prudent when choosing the approach to take as he preached to the crowds before him, when to preach, and when to keep silent. St. Paul was not a man of careless actions—if he was, he would never have been successful. He knew how to adjust his behaviors appropriately in order to live with the wealthy and to live with the poor. He adjusted his way of life in order to not give offense to those to whom he was sent, becoming all things to all men so that he might save some. He made choices, narrowed down possibilities, and acted in the light of what seemed right to him.

The secret of St. Paul's decision making is the same for anyone in leadership, but he coaches us to go about it in a different way. For Paul, the only truly unredeemable decision is the refusal to make one. Sometimes, St. Paul's decisions were not sanctioned by God, and yet not only did God allow him to make them, but he directed him to try again. Think of the time, for example, when St. Paul decided to preach in Asia (see Acts 16:6). He thought about it, decided for it, and made plans to move in that direction, only to have none less than the Holy Spirit prevent him from preaching there (see Acts 16:6). So, he tried again, this time discerning and making plans to preach in Bithynia, only to find that "the Spirit of Jesus did not allow them" (Acts 16:7). What did Paul do in the face of this? He tried again, this time going to Philippi whence God would open all of Europe to the Gospel. Sometimes, St. Paul had to decide without certainty. He had to rely on the Holy Spirit, even when the Holy Spirit course-corrected decisions upon which he had set his heart.

Perhaps this is a key lesson from St. Paul for us—we need to be ready to make mistakes and shift course. We do not know the full extent of God's plans for our lives, why he wants us to pass through some valleys and climb the mountains we need to climb. Yet, without a doubt, God wants us to have the dignity of trying to please him by engaging our free will in the best way we can. Wanting God's will to be done is the first step; the next one is the hard one—trying to engage our will to accomplish his in the best way we can. Like St. Paul, we don't always see our way. Like St. Paul, we will sometimes err and come up short, again and again. And, like St. Paul, we must never stop trying. Sometimes, we have to make choices about our paths with very little light, but if we make them with trust in God and humility of heart, we bear witness to the world of another light coming from someone more powerful than ourselves, the light of a God who can write straight with crooked lines. Isn't that a witness the world desperately needs? By plodding ahead, day after day, where love leads us, we testify to the world that there is someone greater than the world—one who holds the whole world in his hands.

Think of the life of St. Junipero Serra, for instance. When he was sent to help found the mission churches in California, he was sent to bring the Church where there was none. He had to brave hostility, danger, bad weather, and thousands of miles of unmarked terrain to do something no one had done before him. As he did so, he faced situations no one could have foreseen, many of which came with grave consequences. He surely made many mistakes as he did so, but he left us with a personal motto that speaks volumes to what it means to walk with Christian Clarity: "Forward. Always forward."

The example of St. Junipero Serra shows us the difference St. Paul's coaching can make in our lives. Mistakes, confusion, and uncertainty accompany everyone through life. But, if we keep moving forward, making the best choices we can with the light that we have, we find ourselves in the driver's seat in life—and God is always able to make the best of whatever may come our way. To do this, though, we, like St. Paul, have to abandon any plan for approval from those who would judge us based on the standards of worldly perfection. No one who endeavors to lead an intentional, impactful life will do so without imperfection. A true leader in Christ fears something more than being judged by those who stand around them—they fear losing the love that burns within them. And so, coached by Paul, humble and courageous, they take the step that matters most: the next one.

Following Paul's courageous example in the presence of the obscurity of knowing God's will perfectly, we can find a light in the darkness of unknowing. This light comes from the freedom that God has placed in our hearts to glorify him by personally and intentionally choosing to love him in the ways that seem best for our time and place. Coached by Paul, we learn not to be afraid of the fog. We learn to trust in God. We learn to tread boldly forward in faith!

Pondering with Paul . . .

Key points

1.　Having problems is not our main problem. Having problems with having problems—that is the real problem. And it goes the same for being afraid to make a decision. What is causing my fear about deciding? What can I do about it?
   A thought from St. Paul: 1 Corinthians 2:6-10

2.　St. Paul chose to move forward on his mission without always knowing that he was doing the right thing. What enabled him to have this confidence? What would my life look like if I followed Paul's example?
   Read Acts 16:6-10

3.　Not making a decision is still a decision. Are there areas in my life where not deciding has led to undesirable consequences? Can I do anything to change that?
   Read Romans 8:12-17

Six

Jumping

The man leans against the bulkhead of the boat as it quietly slips through the dawn into the port city of Neapolis. His pensive figure peers into the smooth black water, watching as his ship's bow makes the water fold, shine, and disappear again with each thrust of the ship's oars. His companions are busy elsewhere, but Paul cannot stop watching the water and the approaching shoreline. Abruptly, in the strange way customary to the sea, the port's quay appears to race toward the vessel, the sailors make ready to dock, and they are there. Paul remains still, staring steadily down at the water. Only a fist-sized gap now remains between his boat and the dock, between sailing and disembarkation, between Asia and Europe, between him and his future. He can see the reflection of his face in the black water, staring back at him as he watches it move on the water. His thoughts come from within him like sounds from a deep, still well: "What would happen if I went home? What will happen if I go forward? If I walk across this small gap of water onto the pier, what will my life become? Is this really what I need to be doing?" His questions seem like they will string on forever when Paul feels a gentle tugging on his cloak. He turns to see Timothy, satchel in hand, smiling from ear to ear, eager and bright for the journey ahead. Paul knows that, for whatever questions he might have, the time has come. He smiles gently back at his young companion, shoulders the weight of his pack, and steps boldly across the gap. The evangelization of Europe has begun.[10]

And the Lord said to Paul one night in a vision, "Do not be afraid, but speak and do not be silent; for I am with you . . ."

ACTS 18:9-10

Sometimes it can feel difficult to relate to St. Paul and his unflinching heroism (more on that later), but he had to face the same fears we do. Imagine that you are seven years old and standing on a diving board at your local community pool. You are not sure how you got there, but you see for sure that there is only one way down—you have to jump! That would be fine, you suppose, thinking to yourself, except that jumping also means falling, and falling means being terrified for a brief moment, and being terrified for a brief moment is not exactly your definition of fun!

Yet, there you are, shivering and wet, looking down over your toes into the blue water below, wondering what other options there might be. Your brothers are climbing the ladder behind you and begin to make complaining noises about hurrying up and such. Your older sister is standing next to the pool and begins to offer cheering encouragement about how "you can do it," and "just jump!" and other such pleas that begin to jumble around

10. Inspired by Acts 16:10.

in your mind. Time is ticking, and no wishing can change the decision that lies before you—you will either jump into the pool and become a hero (of sorts) or turn around and go back to where you were safe before and face the unbridled mockery of your brothers and their friends.

As isolated as this moment may appear, the fact is, we are presented with the same decision thousands of times per day: we know what we want to do, but will we actually do it? Whether we like it or not, choosing a course of action to follow in order to fulfill our desires is not an adequate recipe for success; once we make a plan about how we want to proceed, we need to act on our chosen course. Every time we pass from planning into action, we are forced to pass through something like a doorway that links our inner world of intention to the outer world of action—a command that our mind makes to our will: *do this.* The ancients had a Latin term for this action, naming it *imperium* (the Latin word for "command"). For some—typically those whose lives are marked by the ability to stay active and productive—this command is second nature; for others—typically, those whose lives are marked by dreamy wishes and unfulfilled hopes— giving this command to themselves triggers a fear that makes stopping look a lot more desirable than engaging. Sometimes, after all, it's easier to just "do for the sake of doing" than really act with intention and choice.

Indeed, we all need to overcome the legitimate fears that can come when we begin new things. When we were little, the first day of school usually came with its fair share of social anxieties. The same held true when we went on our first date or drove the car alone for the first time. One needs to overcome a lot of fear to step out of a hot air balloon with a parachute on, free-falling thousands of feet over the face of the earth. It takes courage to invest your retirement into a financial product knowing that there is always a possibility that the economy will collapse. Whatever it is that we decide to do, great or small, the road to any kind of success in our lives is the same—we need to pass out of the warm womb of our aspirations and dreams into the cold air of reality.

And this is where many of us stall. In some, it might be because of a proclivity to laziness. In others, the passive-aggressive people of the world, it might be because it's the only way that we know how to resolve conflict. It might even be just because we are not convinced that our action plan is a good one and so we are afraid of failure. After all, we cannot be judged by what we *did not* say or do, but we will be judged by everything that we said or did. Once we begin a project, who will protect us from failing at it? There are many reasons that we may pause at the edge of a decision and look down. Whatever the reason is, we need to confront our fears and overcome them or else our dreams will stay what they are: *things that don't exist!*

In truth, for all its inherent insecurity and risk, passing from desire into action remains the only way for our inner freedom to become love in action. Staying safe is an important consideration for our long-term sustainability, but it makes for a dreadful rule for life. Safety and the comfort of the status quo might seem appealing to those who are weighed down by the worries of life, but they can also work a suffocating effect on our souls. No mighty tree of the forest reached its majesty by remaining a seed in the ground. It had to endure the real threats of winds and storms and competition from other trees to reach real heights. Similarly, no human heart that refuses to hammer its red-hot aspirations into the sharpened steel of real attempts can ever radiate its love onto others.

Passing from intention into action reminds us of the scene in the Gospels when St. Peter walked on water. What was St. Peter looking for when he asked Jesus to call him out of the boat to walk on the stormy sea? (see Mt 14:22-31). What could possibly have been on the water that was not found in the boat? In the boat, he had safety and companionship; on the perilous waves, though, he could experience something else—the authenticity of a real love simultaneously fraught with and blessed with real consequence. And so, surprising as it may seem, he thought it preferable to walk bravely on water and face danger than to stay in the boat, secure in his fear.

It was the same for St. Paul. While he never walked on water like St. Peter, there were plenty of times that he got out of boats—moving from one land to another across the seas. And, with each crossing, he had to leave behind the security of where he had been and begin something new. Each time he packed his bag in one city, he knew he would be opening it in another. Every time he got into a boat in one country, he knew that he would have to step off it again in a foreign land. He knew that all his "hellos" would one day be turned into "goodbyes." He accepted that following Christ on the road to heaven by his actions meant that life would constantly change. He accepted that change was a Christian's earthly home.

In some ways, our modern culture does not help us on this point. Sometimes, it plays into our fears, encouraging our insecurities about being able to deal with real consequences in our lives. So, we are taught to protect against them instead. In a culture where we can insure everything against the threat of change—from our cars to our homes to our online identities—and our relationships are built and lost on the virtual platforms of images and screens, we are incentivized to live life in a way that minimizes real risk. We learn to protect ourselves by staying in the "herd" of groupthink and common opinion. There is objectively nothing wrong with following opinions, of course—especially if they are correct! The problem comes, though, when the herd we are following has led us to the wrong place and the commonly held opinion turns out to be just plain wrong. In that case, ironically, our choice to find safety by not taking a stance can bring with it the unintended result of even greater insecurity!

It is no accident that the passage in the Acts of the Apostles that describes St. Paul and Barnabas being sent on their first missionary journey begins with the powerful expression: "So, being sent out by the Holy Spirit . . ." (see Acts 13:4ff). This simple sentence says so much. It shows that the Holy Spirit, our God, *sends* us into action. There is a time for inspiration and desire; there is a time for hesitation, testing, counsel, and discernment. But, once a pathway to action is chosen, we need to walk on it. The apostles are more than nice people whose emotions and sentiments have been soothed by the truth of the Faith; they are men who are *sent by the Holy Spirit* to impact the world around them so that through their real actions, the power of the truth really may be made known. Maybe this is why the Catholic Mass finishes with the command: "Go in peace." We "go" because we are called to speak, to write, to pray, to proclaim, to fast—indeed, even to fail in the eyes of the world! But, in everything we do and in whatever state of life God calls us to, we are sent to be God's instruments—allowing him to influence the world where he sends us regardless of the necessary sacrifices this will require from our resources, friendships, and level of comfort.

It is important to remember, of course, that action is about much more than taking risks; action is even more about what we gain and give by it. Moving into action allows what is in our hearts to become visible, and the beautiful treasures we hold within our souls to become gifts in the lives of others. By doing the deeds we wish were done, we become instruments of God in our world—healing, nourishing, guiding, uplifting one another. What an incredible thought—that God wants to show the world his love by giving it ours! What a privilege to be in a place where we can influence the world for what is good and beautiful and true! From fathers who have the opportunity to teach their sons to be bold and brave and to stand for what is right, to small business owners who can exercise their freedom to create businesses that uplift and purify the culture of their towns, to politicians who can shape public policy to ensure the harmony of success—the possibility of a world that advances toward the kingdom of God lies in the hearts of Christians who dare to impact it with the love of God.

For all of us, passing into action requires this kind of daring. True enough, when we do something ourselves, instead of just commenting on (and criticizing) the doings of others, we become vulnerable to failure and susceptible to criticism by others around us. Starting any new project renders our long-cherished private aspirations open to the kind of judgment that could negatively impact our reputations and shape our options for the future. On the other hand, it is also true that daring to act gives us a gift we would never possess if we chose to listen to the voice of cowardice: the warmth of hope. After all, instead of merely talking about the good things that might be, those who begin to act on their plans are able to point to actual and real success.

St. Paul can coach us here as well. Sometimes, especially in noble Christian souls, the power of the ideals we want to make real is so attractive that we don't begin to make them a reality because the fact that we can only do one thing at a time just seems too small a thing. Focusing on what is in front of us just does not seem adequate to the vision of everything we would like to accomplish. Surely, St. Paul also had a vast vision of what he wanted to accomplish for Christ; and yet, he understood that the only way to bring the world to Christ was by bringing the people in front of him to Christ. We see him, for example, in Athens on the street, speaking literally to anyone who would listen to him about Jesus (see Acts 17:17). And again, we see him in Ephesus, spending the majority of his time teaching a relatively small group of his disciples—anyone who would listen—about the Gospel (see Acts 19:9-10). His biggest difference was not made by addressing large crowds; his biggest impact was made in the depths of the souls of the few in whom he invested every day.

By making the painful sacrifice of the many *possible* ways he could love (however grandiose they might potentially be) in favor of the *one* thing that he could do, he teaches us how to pass from the immaturity of inconsequential wishing into the powerful strides of spiritual adulthood. Instead of aimlessly questioning where the right path could be, we can follow his example and begin to tread upon the path before us with bold steps. The limitations of reality may require us to sacrifice much of the perfection of an ideal that exists as a beautiful dream in our minds, but engaging our circumstantial limitations with real action can yield something even greater than perfection: actual goodness.

Watching St. Paul in action, we notice something else. St. Paul had a strategy and a kind of plan, and yet *he was ready to pivot* depending on what he found in front of him. Embarking on a new adventure means much more than executing a plan perfectly. Paul's example coaches us to remember that good plans are dynamic—we have to be as ready to change and be flexible in order to achieve our goal as we are willing to take the time to prepare for what may come our way.

We see this flexibility clearly when Paul arrives in Philippi (see Acts 16:11ff). He had just walked some five hundred miles by foot across modern-day Turkey without making a single baptism, then had taken a sailing vessel through the sea, and set foot in Europe for the first time. Once there, however, he could not follow his customary strategy of preaching (his usual plan) in a synagogue, because *there was no synagogue in Philippi.* So, instead, on the Sabbath, he went down by the river to pray. There, he sees a group of devout women praying also. Braving the possibility of rejection, and without any real plan, he approaches them and begins to discuss religion with them, sharing his faith. Since he had already fully committed to his mission and put it into action, he had the advantage of being able respond to the situation creatively to match the contours of reality as they come. As he does so, he converts—and then baptizes—St. Lydia, the first Christian in Europe.

St. Paul was intelligent. He knew the value of planning and strategy; however, he was also *determined to accomplish his mission* come what may. What is more, St. Paul teaches us a valuable lesson: *every step forward changes the playing field.* By moving forward, acting on our choices and then regrouping to make new ones, we become the protagonist of our life's stories—we play offense instead of defense. Discovering the hidden paths of possibility is impossible only for those who refuse to try.

Reading the Acts of the Apostles is like reading the story of the Church's victorious conquest, although if we look carefully, we cannot help but notice that the Church's victories in Acts—carried out largely by St. Paul—were victories that came at the cost of a lot of suffering, frustrations, and roadblocks. His life sometimes resembled a ball in a pinball machine! St. Paul was refused, rejected, and chased away from many opportunities, but he kept moving forward, choosing to look for and act upon new opportunities as the Holy Spirit led him. This readiness to act and move made St. Paul a protagonist in the Church's conquest: he was able to find a way to turn whatever situation that he was in into something positive for Christ. He braved the fears of risk and failure, boasting of the weaknesses of the unforeseeable, and so allowed God to bless his world and our lives with an example of what we could express by the term Christian Courage. When, like Paul, we face our challenges with the courage that comes from Christ, the obstacles we face do not block our paths—they point us to the way of victory God plans for us.

Pondering with Paul . . .

Key points

1. To do anything, we have to start. Sometimes, starting is the hardest of things. What could I do before I try to start something that would make starting even easier? What small step could help me make the bigger step I need to make?
    A thought from St. Paul: Acts 13:1-4

2. St. Paul was always ready to pivot in order to keep moving forward. Is God asking me to pivot in my life? What do I need to change to keep moving forward?
    Read Acts 18:1-11

3. Action can be a leader's best friend, because it changes the playing field around us and enables us to find new options and pathways forward. What is one thing within my reach to do that would make the biggest difference for my life?
    Read Acts 22:30 - 23:11

Seven

In Pain, a Name

He could still see them there—their swollen faces, flushed with wine, staring at him in the evening sun through half-closed eyes. He had addressed thousands of people in his years as a proponent of the Gospel. He knew how to read a crowd. And this one was dead. From where he stood on the Acropolis, Paul could see the temple of Athena silhouetted against the sky—mighty, exalted, overflowing with visitors. His audience, he knew, depended financially and otherwise upon the worship of the goddess who gave their city its name, but he had come there to tell them about a different ruler, a God whose name they did not know. He had proposed something new—a truth that would have required them to change everything for the better, but they did not care.

Paul was weary that day as he trudged down the steep path leading away from the giant rock where the rulers of Athens had held their council. He had heard them scoffing at him, had felt the edgy sarcasm in their voices as they dismissed him from their hearing, had seen them quickly turning away from him back to their refreshments and games. How could men of such importance and caliber not even give ear to a truth so profound and convincing? How could men of such power not even care to listen to an argument of such persuasive force? He had made his best case—just as he so often did. He thought that he had seen some flicker of understanding light up the eyes of one or two of them as they sat there. And yet, once again, it had failed to make a real dent on his audience. It was as if they were paralyzed. He had been rejected before, numerous times. This day's rejection only seemed to add to the crushing weight of the burden of failure he carried on his back. He slowly trudged home from the Areopagus that night, his throat sore from preaching, his heart lonely. Lying on his bed he could not sleep—his ears echoing the laughter of men on the hill, and his mind staring bleakly at the stone wall of human rejection rising before him.[11]

We are afflicted in every way, but not crushed; perplexed, but not driven to despair; persecuted, but not forsaken; struck down, but not destroyed . . .

2 CORINTHIANS 4:8-9

Leadership talks and motivational speeches are all the rage these days. Whether from podcasts or radio talk shows, from books or videos, our modern public is ready to consume messages that challenge, inspire, and push us to action. It all seems wonderful—imagining ourselves fit, healthy, educated, leading our businesses—until we try it.

Anyone who has chosen to act on their dreams knows the feeling well—the biting chill of "the grind." It is one

11. Inspired by Acts 17:22-31.

thing to dare to dream, just as it is surely a good thing to plan and choose a course of action. It is a marvel to launch out into the deep and begin an adventure; however, it is an altogether special thing to grind out what it takes to succeed, day after day, no matter what the cost. Many people want to live a genuine Christian life; some even try to do it. However, few are they, it seems, who are willing to do the real, hard work that following Christ will demand from them. Anyone who wants to lead in their sphere of influence has to be willing to pay the price of grinding through the pain that comes as they do so.

It takes courage to push through pain and the risk of burnout is real. If we are not careful, the fear of what our love will cost us every day or of burning out along the way can paralyze us. No one wants to lose themselves or what belongs to them—their beauty, their energy, their time, the opportunities they have to enjoy the pleasures of life. Regardless of the vocation in which we find ourselves, married or consecrated, the daily struggle of fidelity to the duties love requires from us can be very taxing. Obviously, it is important not to confuse what we describe as the Paralysis of Fatigue with emotional or psychological burnout. What is commonly referred to as "burnout" is a real problem with its own set of rules that create their own parameters for our prudence. The answer to feeling high degrees of anxiety, depression, and loss of energy is rarely to increase our energy output and drive ourselves even harder. Instead, we have to learn to respect our limitations, adjust our actions, and incorporate the rest and diversion we legitimately need as limited creatures. The Paralysis of Fatigue we are describing here is much more a question of what is spiritual within us. It comes about when we succumb to the inner calculations of loss and gain to the point where we lose sight of the value of what we will gain in the face of the realization of the sacrifices we make to get there. Think of it in terms of a mountain climber who has endeavored to climb a high mountain. He prepares for the climb, purchases his gear, and happily embarks on his journey. With time, however, having endured rain, bugs, fog, and lightning, with lungs weary and legs worn, he wonders whether the view he so desired is worth the pain he is enduring. He could rest a while, he could regain his strength, or he could slow down, but his is a deeper question: Is the view really worth the climb? If he gives up, he will never know; only by finding a way to prudently measure his strength and get to the top will he ever find out.

Although sometimes, let's face it, the grind can be fun, too. When we are able to focus and gain momentum we can resemble a ship at full steam. Doing things allows us to pick up energy and advance joyfully from one goal to another without being overwhelmed. It can be a lot of fun to make progress and see our desires advance. But, at other times, we meet with opposition—things don't go our way and the currents pushing against us can seem stronger than our will to swim through them. Our feet feel like they are trudging through mud, and we risk getting stuck. Slowly, instead of drawing in the spiritual oxygen of renewed desire, we can feel like we are suffocating and we start to calculate the cost of our efforts against the goal we wish to achieve. "Is this really worth it?" we ask ourselves. "Is the view worth the climb?" If we allow our fears about what we lose in daring great things grip us, we can begin to slow down, lose momentum, and, often enough, grind to a halt. In our ministry, we like to call this surrender to the fear of paying the price for what we hope to gain the Paralysis of Fatigue. Obviously, it is important not to confuse what we describe as the Paralysis of Fatigue with emotional or psychological burnout, even though the two are often intertwined.

What, then, is the secret of saints like Paul? How did he keep going for forty years at such a pace and not quit? How did he push through the pain of what he lost in service to God?

Remember one of the fundamental axioms of Christian leadership: having problems is not the problem. Having problems with having problems—that's the real problem. St. Paul had problems surrounding the toil and labor his love required of him, but he coaches us to approach them less as problems and more as opportunities. The fact that effectively accomplishing things can be sometimes painful, costing us energy and time that we will never get back, does not have to be viewed as a negative thing. In fact, from those who embrace leadership with the grace of Christ as St. Paul did, the grind that accompanies action becomes the indispensable and cherished language of their love for others or desire to accomplish their goal, just as the Cross was the language of God's love for the world. This was the secret behind the constancy of St. Paul. He learned to unite his sufferings with the sufferings of Jesus as a prayer for his followers—a prayer that would become a gift of grace, saving them (see 2 Cor 1). In fact, his labors for the Church, with their accompanying pain, became actual sources of joy for him. He even boasts of them (see 2 Cor 12), holding his head high as he suffered to fulfill his mission.

Something similar to St. Paul's mindset in the midst of his activities exists in the realm of music. It is called circular breathing—allowing air to be exhaled from the body at the same time as air is inhaled into the lungs. Wind musicians trained in this technique are able to sustain the sound from their instruments over very long periods of time without stopping to take a breath. Amazingly, by simultaneously breathing out and breathing in, they are able to continue their sound without running out of oxygen. They are just like veteran married couples who have learned how to transform their daily tasks into moments of encounter and discovery, or sailors who learn to prefer the hard life they live at sea to the easy life at port by filling their time on board with activities uniquely their own. Saints like St. Paul teach us to find and embrace the spiritual value hidden within the grind like a precious pearl. Just as musicians learn to inhale while they exhale, Christians learn to spiritually benefit from what they lose for others. We learn to give cheerfully even when it comes at a cost. This is the essence of what we can call Christian Constancy and it is the blessing God gives the world when we persevere through the pain of "the grind" by his grace.

So, what kind of spiritual gain does St. Paul tell us we can expect by expending our efforts in the pursuit of fulfilling our vocation? He coaches us to keep our eyes on our spiritual prize. The grind gives something we could never achieve without it—our true identity emerges, and we claim our name. Think of it this way: God made us who we are, giving us an identity as unique and unrepeatable as our name. When our actions flow from that deep identity (out of the inimitable person God made us to be—uniquely good, singularly loving, and wonderfully creative), we glorify God, blessing the world he made by making his image and likeness visible in ourselves. When we act from the heart—according to the individual "name" we received from God—we reflect God's beauty onto our world in a way as uniquely inspiring as our own identity.

We could never fully measure the power behind the truth that our souls (our hearts, minds, and freedom) were made directly by God in his image and likeness. It means that each one of us brings God's glory directly into our world when we engage our freedom and act as love directs us. It is true that this action will always imply expending our resources—"dying" on the outside, if you will—but at the same time as bringing us into "the grind," our actions cause us to expand on the inside. We literally become ourselves more and more by choosing to act in accord with God's love, allowing our identity to impact the world around us throughout our lives. Our loss is our pain, but in the grind we discover our name.

Is it any wonder, then, that God chose the labor and pain that come with following our vocation as the place where he would work the wonder of his redemption in us and others? Even as his life demonstrates Christian Constancy, St. Paul teaches us that the grind of our labors can be more than productive—it can be *redemptive*. The suffering of sacrifice is a tool in God's hand that he uses to chisel away at our own attachment to selfishness and evil, as we work out our salvation with "fear and trembling"

(Phil 2:12). And, even more, Paul also teaches us that by embracing the grind for his glory, we can win grace for others (see 2 Cor 1:6). Literally, just as an earthly mom or dad shows their parenthood by providing for their children, so we are called to be spiritual fathers and mothers by winning grace for others through the labors of our state in life. We do this by embracing our crosses with Jesus and uniting our suffering to his in prayer. All of us who struggle under a heavy load in life can learn from St. Paul's attitude: "[I]n my flesh I complete what is lacking in Christ's afflictions" (Col 1:24). And, just like a musician's method of circular breathing, because he labored in union with Christ and his sacred Passion, the high cost he really paid to be a spiritual father turned into the very thing that pushed him forward to finish his race.

At its root, St. Paul's coaching to those who are bearing the intensity of labor can be summed up in one word: *alignment.* The inner paralysis we call the Paralysis of Fatigue that comes from fearing the cost of the sacrifice love can require comes in two phases. And so, we need to discover two kinds of alignment: the first, an alignment to allow God's grace to transform our daily efforts into the instrument of his redemption; the second, to transform the losses we embrace for his sake into glory. The first alignment—the alignment between our deepest identity, our freedom, and the actions we need to perform every

day—will be covered in this chapter. The second kind of
alignment—the alignment between these same actions and
our highest purpose—we will look at in the next chapter.
When we let St. Paul show us how to embrace these two
kinds of inner alignments, our daily actions form a bridge
between our identity and our transcendent purpose like
a bridge over the troubled waters of life. However, just as
surely as a bridge will collapse if its pillars crack and fail,
so we will encounter crushing burnout when either of
these two alignments bends out of shape.

This transformation in accordance with our true
identity is not easy for any of us, and it was not easy for
Paul, either. He had to learn to glory in the sufferings
that he endured for Christ—transforming his losses into
conduits for Christ's blessings to flow through him—or
else he would have collapsed under their sheer weight.
Not only did he walk over ten thousand miles—through
mosquito-laden marshes, dry deserts, and rocky mountain
roads—but he did so while constantly being in danger.
Highway robbers abounded, wild beasts lurked in the
bushes, streams and floods could swallow him up as he
crossed them, and once he was even bitten by a poisonous
snake. He was exposed to freezing cold and blistering sun,
rebuffed by winds and soaked by rains. And, when he
sailed the seas, we know that he was shipwrecked twice at
least—one time when a terrible storm stranded him for a

month on the Isle of Malta, and another when he drifted for a day and a half treading water in the open sea.

And that's not all. St. Paul did his job under the constant pressure of fierce hostility. Besides the "false brethren" (2 Cor 11:26) who were present when he taught, ready to betray him with false accusations, he was the object of at least five riots so violent that onlookers were "afraid that [Paul] would be torn in pieces" by the crowds (Acts 23:10). He was scourged three times, whipped five times, beaten with rods three times, and even stoned once and left for dead. He was imprisoned for years at a time—without a trial— hunted down by men bearing knives with which to stab him, sought after by a band of forty assassins who had sworn not to eat or drink before killing him, driven out of cities by their townsmen, scoffed at by leading intellectuals, and abandoned by his own companions. And yet, because he did it for Christ, as a gift from his heart, even while he endured all of this, Christ strengthened him—the grace of Christ kept Paul constant. By God's power working within him during all of this outer weakness and trouble, Paul founded some twenty church communities, wrote thirteen books of the New Testament, brought life to countless souls, and spread a faith that continues to this day.

Is it any wonder then, that you and I have to face the hardships of the daily grind? It is safe to say that if God did not want us to make our love real and our hearts grow through sweat and perseverance, he would have created a different plan. It was not by chance that when he came to the earth, he came as a tradesman and shouldered the burden of providing for and caring for his mother. Nor was it by chance that Paul's efforts to plant the cross in every land were to prove so costly. Perhaps the real problem is not that our love requires toil to become real. Perhaps the real problem is that we don't see our toil as the true gift that it is.

The way that St. Paul approached the real sufferings in his life as a leader reveals an astonishing truth— the more that he gave himself away through the daily hardships of the work God had called him to do, the more he became the man God had made him to be. His action, freely chosen by him as a gift to God and to his flock—even though it cost him the strength of his youth and the comforts of his old age—allowed him to truly become the man God had intended him to be. He led with real actions, given from his real heart, one after the other, day after day, paying for his love by bearing real scars upon his back, consuming real energy, and spending real time that he could never gain back for himself. And, somewhere in the grind of forty years of living what was a "daily death" (see 1 Cor 15:31), his identity became as real as his action. In the grind, he found his name. Deep within Paul's sacrifices, God was at work—gradually transforming Paul into whom God created him to be: an apostle of Christ Jesus.

When we give our toil to Jesus as a gift of love from the heart, we discover the deep power of the Christian life—aligning our name with what we do gives us *integrity*. Integrity allows our work to express our love even as our love fuels our work. And, as we work with integrity, our work becomes the place of God's work in the world as well. St. Paul had found the way to see his daily ministering of the Gospel as the truest expression of who he was. "[I]t is no longer I who live, but Christ who lives in me" (Gal 2:20). Could there be any loftier aspiration for the way that we look at our lives, our work, and our toil, than to see our efforts to lift up the world around us somehow bearing in them the influence and blessing of Jesus Christ? It's an alluring perspective, to say the least. Instead of allowing our secular world to define how we view the daily hardships of toil and effort that make up our careers and homelife, St. Paul teaches us to view them as a mission from God through which God can bless our world. What a thought: to see yourself as God's gift to nursing, God's gift to banking, God's gift to your children, and to see the price you pay for the happiness you seek as God's gift to you. It's a perspective that changes everything by aligning everything with the most essential of things.

The truth is, each of us was made uniquely by God from within an unrepeatable act of love. God did not make us because he needed to; he did not make us because in some way we made him any better. He made us out of his sheer good pleasure, *because he wanted us to exist.* He literally loved us into being. When we pray, we love him back. When we love him back, we transform all we go through into that prayer. Maybe this is why Paul coaches us on how to pray. Not only does he teach us to pray by asking God to help others and give thanks for them, but he bids us to pray for ourselves—that our lives might be peaceful and quiet, dignified and godly. Paul saw great value in prayer, bidding us to "pray constantly, give thanks in all circumstances" (1 Thes 5:17-18) even if "we do not know how to pray as we ought" (Rom 8:26).

He also coaches us that pushing through the pain our labors cost us requires a lot of common sense. Even our Lord took time to recharge his strength, offering us an example. He slept on a cushion while on board the boat with his twelve apostles. He sat down by a well in the heat of the day to rest. He slipped away by himself to the mountains to pray, and he enjoyed a meal with Martha, Mary, and Lazarus just before his Passion. St. Paul, too, describes the joy of his many friendships—with Jason, Priscilla and Aquila, Barnabas and Luke among many others—and is unabashed about his affection for some of the communities he founded, longing to be with them again and to enjoy their fellowship. He spent much of his time in prayer, made sure to have periods of rest, and was able to spend time alone. If we are going to stretch ourselves through demanding, challenging activity, we need to take the time to be centered and healthy.

In a surprising way, St. Paul came to love the same grind that cost him so much. He wrote to Timothy that he was happy to be poured out "like a libation" (2 Tm 4:6)[12] for others because he knew that his sacrifices would benefit them and help them make progress in their faith. St. Paul believed his sufferings would be fruitful. He referred to himself as a father through his efforts, said that he was "in labor" (Gal 4:19)[13] to give life for those to whom he preached, and described himself as a teacher, a farmer waiting for growth, and a master builder. He learned not to look *at* the suffering that his life would entail, but to look *through* it—at the faces, the names, and the lives of those for whom he chose to lay it down. He offered his suffering as a gift for those he loved, and teaches us to do the same.

---

12. NABRE translation.
13. NABRE translation.

Pondering with Paul . . .

Key points

1.   The fact that accomplishing things is hard does not have to be a negative thing. In fact, St. Paul shows us that it is an opportunity to glorify God. Are there hard things in my life that I can look at differently in this light?
     A thought from St. Paul: 1 Corinthians 15:58

2.   God has placed each of us in the world to glorify him there. A key to surviving the daily grind is to align our labors with our identity. How do I see myself? What would change in the way I lived if I let myself believe that God was pleased with me in the way I was living out my vocation?
     Read 2 Corinthians 4:1-18

3.   The grind can cause burnout. We need to take care of ourselves and rest as well and as much as we need to persevere through our challenges. Where is God opening a door for me to find him and be refreshed on my journey?
     Read Romans 15:30-33

Eight

In Loss, Gain

A single shaft of the morning sun pierces the tiny window. It slowly crawls across a cold stone floor, eventually revealing a man slumped in the corner, and causing him to slowly raise his head from slumber. As if on cue, the muffled din of soldiers and servants milling about their morning routine slowly begins to fill the small cell. Paul smirks and chuckles to himself thinking of how used he's become to this. He thinks back to that first time in prison in Philippi singing praises with Timothy through the night and realizes that he's somehow grown accustomed to these small spaces. He had been in them many times before, but this time was different.

"Thank God for nephews!" Paul thought to himself wryly, stroking his beard as he rose and meandered to the door of his cell. He had always loved his sister's son, but never had he thought that the lad would save his life! From his position, sitting in chains, collared in the barracks of the Roman cohort garrisoned in Jerusalem, he was entirely at the mercy of a system that cared as much about justice as it did about his fate. No system would save him, he realized, but his nephew might! With a hush, his nephew had told him about a plot hatched by forty assassins who laid in wait to kill him on his way to his next hearing. With a rush, Paul had dispatched his nephew to report all that he knew to the centurion in charge.

Provisions had been made to protect him, but as Paul now stood at the door, ready to be transported on a journey that could mean his death, he felt the familiar fingers of fear slide around his heart. Staying here certainly would mean his death at the hands of his own people. Going forward might mean death at the hands of a force lying in wait along the dark sides of the road. But arriving at his goal would surely lead to his death at the hands of a legal system plagued by corruption and treachery. He sighed and closed his eyes. It was a lot to take in.

He had been here before, at the portals of death, and he had found a way around them every time. This time, however, was different. The one who had sent him there, the Lord who had asked him to bear witness to him by his life, now had asked him to bear witness to him by his death. And so, the Paul who had climbed mountains and sailed seas in service to his Jesus would have to make one final journey—one from which there would be no return. Yes, he had been here before, and this time, there was no going around it. Instead, he would go through it, going where his Lord had gone first. Calmly, he opened his eyes, looked up at the waiting horses and soldiers, formed the corners of his mouth into a manly smile, and told them that he was ready to go.[14]

. . . I have suffered the loss of all things, and count them as refuse, in order that I may gain Christ . . .

PHILIPPIANS 3:8

14. Inspired by Acts 23:16-35.

I remember being at a birthday party for a priest who was turning forty-one years old. He was a very active priest, and some of his friends had gathered with him to celebrate with a dinner. The party was in full swing, and right before the time approached to cut the cake, the priest paused and turned to another priest—twenty years his elder—and asked him if he had any words of wisdom to share. The elder priest thought for a moment, looking down to gather his thoughts and then said solemnly, "Beware of the mid-life crisis when it comes." The guests at the party all burst out laughing, knowing full-well that this kind of thing might happen to their priest friend whose ministry had always been so full of activity. Sensing that maybe God was trying to tell him something, the younger priest pressed his friend to share more, asking, "And, when it comes, what should I do?" The older priest replied, simply, "It's hard. Until you come to terms with the fact that you are going to die. Then, it gets easier."

From the time of our youth, through the arc of middle age, our lives follow an upward pattern of growth and expansion. Every year seems to bring new accomplishments with it—new possibilities to expand our prosperity and develop our strength. If we are fortunate, with time, we gain our independence, fall in love, start a family, begin a career, buy a first house, have friends, and find ways to enjoy our prosperity. But, even if we are not blessed with material well-being, most of us still learn things, make new friends, try out our skills, test ourselves, and grow in wisdom. When we are young, our lives seem to have a logic to them—the logic of the order of personal growth and advancement—and its logic is hard to refute, so long as we remain young.

The young undertake new projects with bravado and excitement—like a ship that sets sail for distant ports, full of expectation and ready to meet whatever comes. Something happens, however, as we advance in the pursuit of our goals over the course of our lives—the daily grind chips away at our energy and we begin to realize more and more what we stand to lose if we pursue our dreams. The years spent at work away from home can never be replaced. The sleep we cut back on as we work hard will impact our health. Many opportunities we pass by simply will not come again. We will become the result of our choices—good and bad—and we realize that in some areas, we will no longer be able to choose a different path. To begin things, we need to kindle the fires of desire; to finish them, we will need to fire the furnaces of sacrifice.

This can be scary for many of us. Our modern world, in many ways, celebrates what is soft and easy, and seems to prefer them over things that are costly to attain. The more one lives amidst easy pleasures, the quicker they begin to feel entitled to them and instinctively abhor the sting of sacrifice. It is natural to seek comfort over discomfort, and so we do much of what we do to attain as much comfort as we can. For many, suffering is a problem to be solved instead of a necessity to be embraced as we pursue something greater. Yet, just as we have learned from St. Paul to endure the grind of toil by putting our deep identity into our work, so we can also learn from him that the secret to ultimate endurance comes from aligning our sacrifices and losses with the victories that we could never achieve any other way.

In Greek, St. Paul used a special word for this inner fire that we need in order to succeed. He called it *hupomoné*. It literally means the ability to "stand underneath" the weight of our challenges, and pay the price of victory by enduring the pain it will require. The best translation we have for this word is the blunt English word *grit*. St. Paul loves this concept of steadfast endurance in the face of trials, using this term eighteen times in his writings. He insisted that grit is a necessity for the Christian life because it perfects our faith. In describing the Christian life, St. Paul did not hesitate to use images of grit found in warfare (see Eph 6), athletic competition (see 1 Cor 9:25-26), and heroism (see Col 2:15).

Paul does more than teach us about grit—this strength by which we accept the little "deaths" implied by our choices for the sake of the fruitfulness that they will produce. He teaches us how to develop it. His very life shows us that the secret to endurance lies in what keeps our focus and where we place our aim. In his exploits, he seemed to approach life as if he was aiming at a different goal than the rest of us. Sure, he wanted to achieve practical things through his actions—establish communities, reconcile sinners, instruct the faithful, and such—just the way all of us are focused every day on our families and jobs; but there was something more that drove him. Namely, he loved Christ with an intimate passion. He loved him *personally*—consecrating himself to Jesus alone, body and soul.

Let's remember that Paul had chosen to be celibate out of love for Christ (and wished that everyone else could experience the love of Christ that powerfully as well; see 1 Cor 7:7). This meant that Paul's interior focus was not so much about *what* he was doing. Paul's interior focus— the deep intention of his heart that undergirded all his actions—was all about *why* he was doing what he was doing. He wanted to accomplish whatever he was doing *only* if it was in profound alignment with why he was doing it in the first place. And, for Paul, his *why* was clearly defined: to glorify Jesus Christ in his body and bring others to do the same (see 1 Cor 6:12-20).

This is a profound lesson for us, because it means that St. Paul was willing to see and accept a degree of incompletion—even worldly failure—in *what* he was accomplishing if that setback allowed him better to share in the Passion and Cross of Jesus whom he knew and served and desired. By doing everything out of love for Jesus and in union with him, Paul had found a way to find gain in loss, victory in defeat, life in death. He coaches us to look at our sacrifice by directing our gaze toward the ones for whom we offer it—the ones whom we love and for whom we labor. From this perspective, love is more powerful than the success we naturally strive for, and love can reach its goal even when our efforts fail. That should give us great hope and great freedom. In fact, it seemed that so long as Paul was loving Jesus and sharing the communion of his heart with him, *he was always winning.* It was as if he embraced a mind shift— the Christian wisdom of the Cross—that allowed him to deploy his incredible energies irrevocably, long-term, across a lifetime of varied activities, and even in the face of impending death.

Perhaps it is only when we are forced to stare down death that we realize the real loss we face by dedicating our time and energy to activities and things that do not last. Death—whether in the ultimate sense of the word, or metaphorically—was not the main problem for St. Paul. With his mind renewed by his faith in a crucified king, he saw that his loss was a sharing in the saving and glorious death of Christ. He understood the reality of loss as much as any of us, and demonstrated Christian Constancy by transforming the powerful natural fears it brings with it by making death a gift of love. He coaches us to see our sacrifices as having real value in God's eyes. Our many daily deaths are meaningful to God because by them we offer ourselves to him by acts of love for others.

St. Paul was not paralyzed by the fear of death or sacrifice. After all, Paul went to Jerusalem without hesitation, even though he had been warned three times by the Holy Spirit that going there would be the beginning of his martyrdom for Christ. And this was the same Paul who felt "afflicted in every way, but not crushed; perplexed, but not driven to despair; persecuted, but not forsaken; struck down, but not destroyed" (2 Cor 4:8-9). Paul's perspective shows us the power our faith can have—it aligns the sacrifices of our daily grind with the most meaningful love of our lives: the love of Jesus.

Indeed, nothing seemed to be able to stop St. Paul, because his love stretched beyond and through every obstacle. As he said to the Ephesians, his dear friends, when leaving them for the last time to go to his certain death, "I do not account my life of any value nor as precious to myself, if only I may accomplish my course and the ministry which I received from the Lord Jesus, to testify to the gospel of the grace of God" (Acts 20:24).

On the one hand, the external activities that sapped his life's energies just as they do ours were bearable because they were aligned with his call—the personal freedom expressed by his name. And, on the other hand, his real sacrifices became gifts of life because they were aligned with the true, deep love of his life—Jesus Christ. Just as leaning into Christ's sacred Passion allowed him to find meaning in his toil—and to discover his identity, his "name," in truth—so, the same Passion of Christ allowed him to discover the life-giving power of God that flowed through his sacrifices, his losses, and the many forms of "daily death" he faced in his labors. Could he say it any more succinctly than when he says it to the Colossians? "Now I rejoice in my sufferings for your sake, and in my flesh I complete what is lacking in Christ's afflictions for the sake of his body, that is, the church" (Col 1:24).

Indeed, these are two focal points for the soul of the Christian leader who chooses to dare something great for Christ—just like Paul—wherever God has called them to labor in life. The first focal point is the Lord who claims our heart. Paul saw the sacrifices of his labors as a gift that he made to God out of love. Thanks to the Holy Spirit, his daily deaths became a gift to the Father—"a fragrant offering and sacrifice to God" (Eph 5:2). What St. Paul did, he did to glorify God, not himself. Thanks to the Holy Spirit, the real losses, the real pain, that his dedication to Jesus entailed became a source of consolation (see Gal 6:17), and the basis for his hope for future glory. This reality is the same for us. Our daily vocation is just that—a calling from God to glorify him through the gift of our lives in love poured out. When God asks us to pour ourselves out, St. Paul teaches us to see our sacrifice for what it is: a libation poured out as love for God (see 2 Tm 4:6).

The second focal point of a Christian leader is the good that our sacrifices can do for others. In other words, the fruitfulness of God through our lives. Not only did St. Paul believe that the life he poured out and the energies he lost would unite him to the Jesus he loved, but he took consolation in knowing that he was edifying the Church. Be it through instruction, fellowship, or works of mercy, he also believed that what he was doing was more than something quantifiable; he believed that his life was a channel of God's saving grace. His was not just human constancy; his was Christian Constancy: the constancy of Jesus within him. He was able to connect the labors he had to undertake every day with the salvation of souls he so longed for. And it can be the same for us. The real value of our lives is more than the sum of how many things we have gained for ourselves or the successes we will have accumulated. There is also an incalculable value, hidden and mysterious, in the way we will share and show the love of Jesus in what we do or even in how we failed while daring greatly. Christian leaders act out of a deeper wisdom than anything the human mind can conjure up on its own. They show that a human life can be more than human—when Jesus lays hold of it, it can bear something of the life of God.

Yes, Paul kept his "eyes on the prize." The prize of his heart: to be one with Jesus and to build up the Church. This is the great secret of Christian leadership done in the light of St. Paul. Even though we might feel like the "single grain" that falls to the earth and dies, we do not remain alone! (see Jn 12:24). Mysteriously, the solitude that accompanies our sacrifices becomes fruitful. We pass from mere casual friendship into profound communion. When we lead in love—when we endure the losses of life with Christian grit—we discover the Church for what she truly is: membership in the Body of Christ.

Pondering with Paul . . .

Key points

1. Jesus said we would find our lives by losing them for his sake. What does this mean for me? Whom is Jesus calling me to serve with my life?
    A thought from St. Paul: Philippians 3:12-21

2. God can be glorified by our worldly failure as much as by our success. Where is the cross of Christ in my life? Am I choosing to embrace it?
    Read 2 Timothy 4:1-8

3. One of the keys to perseverance is aligning our labors with the goals we are motivated to achieve by them. Do I have my eyes on the right prize? Whose life is going to be made better by mine?
    Read 2 Timothy 1:1-5

Nine

In Solitude, Friends

The cloak sat warm and soft upon his bony shoulders. Paul was used to being cold and alone, but this winter had just seemed unusually brutal. Maybe it was the solitude of his old age. Maybe it was the trauma that he felt after being imprisoned alone for years without a trial. Maybe it was the sadness that he felt when he remembered the tears of his friends on the docks of Ephesus when he saw them for the last time before setting sail. It could be for any number of reasons, but Paul had been cold in a different way this winter, feeling a kind of frostbite settle its teeth on his heart. Maybe that was why he felt so warm now that Timothy had brought him his cloak. Carrying it with him all the way from Troas, he had placed it with a bright smile and warm embrace across Paul's shoulders, and Paul could feel its warmth— all the way to his heart. The cloak carried on it the scented memories of the evenings he had spent laughing by the fire at the home of Priscilla and Aquila, the smell of roasted lamb rising from the kitchen of Lydia, the soft couches he had enjoyed at the home of Jason while they watched the sunset over the bay of Thessalonica. His shoulders were warmed by his cloak, but his mind was reminded of his friends—the many friends—that he had made as he journeyed on his solitary way. And, as he breathed in the unforgotten scents on the cloak wrapped close under his chin, he could feel the love that came with it, somehow woven deep in its fibers. He was alone, yes. But somehow, his friends were there too. And his heart glowed warm again.[15]

All who are with me send greetings to you. Greet those who love us in the faith.

TITUS 3:15

Let's face it, leadership can be lonely sometimes. Like the prow of a ship, a leader has to break the waves and the ice of their ship's chosen course for the sake of those who will sail gently in the wake their efforts leave behind. It can be uncomfortable to make decisions for our families when we feel like our decisions will make us live differently from everyone else in our group of friends. It can be uncomfortable to try to assert ourselves as parents when we feel like our children do not respect our leadership. It can be uncomfortable to bring other opinions to bear in a society dominated by tyrannical groupthink. It can be uncomfortable to lead.

I remember speaking one time with a priest who shared that, while in seminary, other people considered him to be "holy." He stood out amidst his peers for his silence and devotion. Members of the greater Church community would hold him in esteem because of his religious habit, his title, and his knowledge of the Word

---

15. Inspired by 2 Tm 4:13.

of God. But then, when he started his actual ministry, all of that changed. Faced with the daily stresses, the real anxieties, and the actual opposition that makes up the daily life of the shepherd of God's people, all of his personal weaknesses came to the light. His fits of anger flashed for all to see. He could not keep his frustrations to himself. He unveiled his penchant for gossip and showed that he could complain with the best of them. His leadership, the priest confessed, humbled him much more than he had ever thought possible. "Everyone thought I was holy, until I started to lead them. Now, everyone can plainly see that I am as much a sinner as anyone else!"

The experience, of course, is common to anyone who dares to lead. Once you step out in front, everyone can see your shortcomings. For most, the experience can be so crushing that they try to avoid it by one of two extremes—some choose to deny they have any flaws, and others, convinced of their shortcomings and afraid of the judgment they will incur in the eyes of others, simply refuse to lead at all. What mother wants to wrestle everyday against the will of her truculent child? What husband wants to dare the wrath of his wife's scornful disappointment? What executive wants to be defeated by their company's competition? There are many reasons we may face rejection when we try to influence others, and none of them are fun. Rejection has a singular power to choke our spirits; no one wants to lead people whom they are convinced do not want to follow them.

In our ministry, we like to call the paralysis that comes when we surrender to the fear of rejection by those whom we seek to influence as the Paralysis of Forlornness. It is a kind of fear that spreads outward from the inside, and becomes a self-fulfilling prophecy. People reject us because we act like we will be rejected by them! This makes it a particularly pernicious kind of fear—the longer we make ourselves unlovable, the harder it is to find people to love us, and the circle spirals deeper and deeper. Unlike other obstacles to leadership, forlornness starts inside the leaders themselves. More than any other form of paralysis, it represents the influence of our inner, mental game over our actions. And, oddly enough, the sentiment that what we do has no value in the eyes of those for whom we do it can cripple people who may possess tremendous vision, daring, and grit in every other aspect of leadership. Even greatly talented people can stand oddly forlorn—feeling alone in a sea of people who actually love them.

This is because, in fact, leadership is only *half* about a leader's vision and ability. The other half of leadership is about how effectively a leader can forge a bond with those who follow them. Trust, it turns out, is just as important for reaching our goals as vision and passion.

We all know that we can have the best ideas in the world, and an uncommon ability to fight for what we believe in, but if we cannot win over followers to our cause, our ability and our spirit won't translate into success. Marketers need to touch the hearts of the people they are trying to reach as much as they need analytics. Coaches need to inspire the members of their team to play their best as much as they need to know how to recruit the talent for their team. Managers need to earn the respect of those whom they manage as much as they need to understand their company's operations. Most small organizations make the mistake of confusing competency with leadership. But, in fact, they are two very different things. One skill set is needed to get things done; another skill set—the ability to connect effectively and motivate people—is needed to lead.

Paradoxically, St. Paul shows us that, for a Christian, nothing enables a leader to connect with others more powerfully than embracing the solitude that comes from God's love for the leader. And, strangely enough, this love is often felt most keenly in the weakness of isolation and loneliness. Alone, when we sit in the dark corners of our souls, forced there by the cruel world of rejection, God can still be found. The very Jesus who hung alone, condemned, and ridiculed upon the cross, hung there so that no one would ever be alone again. If we choose to be brave in that pain and hold our heads high, looking for God there, we will find him. Isolation by others can introduce us to a freedom and intensity of love that God alone can give. Courage in the face of the fear of rejection by those we serve can be the vehicle for a unique blessing of God in our world. It is the way that we forge influence based on God's power instead of our own, and we could call it Christian Communion. St. Paul knew this, and provides us with an exceptional example of how a leader can leverage the power of a communion and trust that comes from the love of God that Paul discovered within the solitude that his calling entailed. Indeed, St. Paul had many opportunities to fold in on himself and consider himself unworthy of winning followers. Think of the way that he could have allowed embarrassment to silence him—not only had he personally been responsible for arresting the relatives and friends (a fate possibly resulting in death) of the very people he stood in front of as he proclaimed Christ in synagogues, but he was spending much of his time proclaiming the Messiah's coming as a Jewish rabbi, addressing his fellow Jews in their synagogues. This meant that he was constantly in the awkward position of trying to motivate people to embrace a huge change in their foundational worldview. Anyone who has ever tried cold-calling sales is familiar with this feeling. Salespeople interrupt the course of someone's life to bring them a change that they did not know they needed. And this was St. Paul's business—bringing the unknown to people in a way that made them feel like they wanted something that, in fact, they did not think they wanted. To succeed at his mission, he needed to brave embarrassment and rejection every day.

What is more, St. Paul was in a delicate position. He could not make his proposals from the platform of wealth, power, and secure relationships; instead, he came to them as a poor beggar. As a traveler to their towns, he chose to be hosted by friends for his lodging. Although there were times when he worked and paid for his own living, quite often he was provided for by the generosity of benefactors. And, though that might seem an ideal situation from the outside, the reality of receiving gifts and provisions from others is that it places you in a subordinate position with respect to them. When you receive good things from someone, you owe them a relationship in return. You need to thank them, spend time with them, be attentive to them, and build a relationship with them that you then take with you wherever you go. Over the course of time, these relationships can multiply and even encumber your freedom—be it from the way you need to relax or the way you can express yourself and your opinions. You feel indebted to your friends, and it can be hard to shepherd people to whom you feel indebted. If St. Paul asserted himself so effectively as an apostle of Christ, it could only have come from within the place of meekness and humility that his constant travels and many indebted relationships forced him to acquire.

And all of this was exacerbated by the personality of Paul himself. Paul admits that his presence was not always impressive, and he even put some of his listeners to sleep! People openly struggled to understand his reasoning at times, with someone no less than St. Peter himself commenting that some find his letters "hard to understand" (2 Pt 3:16). Weak as so many of us feel, he even calls himself an "earthen vessel" (2 Cor 4:7) who cannot do what he wants, and usually does what he wishes to avoid (see Rom 7:15-25). He was treated by people who did not know him as a revolutionary, a criminal, and someone who stirs up trouble. He was the object of jealousy, mistreatment, and contempt by people in high places in society. He worked with his hands in businesses owned by others to make enough money to live, and often had to go without even basic needs—mentioning that at times he lacked shelter, clothing, and even food.

And yet, paradoxically, by bravely facing the circumstances that could have caused him to rightly feel forlorn and worthy of rejection, Paul found the strength in Christ to form deep, lasting, authentic relationships. It was as if another power was at work in the midst of his weakness—a power that only a courageous faith in the love of God for him could release. He mentions his many friends by name—individuals whom he greets affectionately—at the ends of his letters, remembering times and places where they walked together in the Lord. And, when it came to Aquila and Priscilla, he not only lived with them, but he worked for them, and eventually converted them to the Lord. They became so close to him that they moved their business from Corinth to Ephesus and helped Paul build up the Church there. Paul knew true friendships with every class and kind of people— with wealthy widows, intellectuals, business owners, slaves, and members of the working class. Even though being without so much of what humanly could make him "strong" in terms of being someone people would choose to follow, God worked through his weakness to produce communities of people that persist even two thousand years later.

Like most leaders who know the gravitational suction of forlornness, he could have suffered the effects of fear of rejection all the more because he was endowed with a truly sensitive heart. Only a heart uniquely thirsty for relationships and approval would so intensely feel their absence. He speaks of the Philippians as being held in his heart as he "yearn[s] for [them] all with the affection of Christ Jesus," thanking God for them every time he thinks of them (Phil 1:3-10). He knelt upon the wharf in Ephesus while his people wept, embracing him and sending him off for the last time. He claims that he is the "father" of the Church in Galatia, and with that same father's love, strongly disciplined the sinful behaviors of the Corinthians.

All of this speaks to Paul's ability to be vulnerable with others. We form relationships by opening ourselves to giving and receiving love with others. And, forlornness strikes at that root of our ability to love by convincing us that we are not fundamentally good. No one wants to give to others (in this case, themselves) something that they perceive to be worthy of rejection. For Paul to be able to form community, he had to be brave in the face of the many conditions in his circumstances where he could feel worthy of being rejected, and give himself anyway. People form community with others when they feel loved by them. Since communities only form where love flourishes, St. Paul could only accomplish his mission to bring the community of the Church to distant places by bringing genuine love into the equation. He had to rely on God for the approval that no social setting could guarantee him, and, based on that reliance, offer the vulnerability necessary to build community. This love he needed to create communion came from God deep inside the solitude he embraced when he faced the objective weaknesses of his life's situation.

Therein lies the whole secret of St. Paul's coaching for those of us feeling the temptation to the Paralysis of Forlornness. He followed Christ repeatedly into positions of weakness, subservience, and even embarrassment, and then he served him there with his whole heart. God laid his sensitivity like a bar of steel on the anvil of the fear of rejection that makes the soul solitary and alone, and he hammered his heart into a chain of love strong enough to bind believers into a Church. Of himself, he was a beggar, a traveler, a worker, hungry, poor, and without finesse. And yet, because he was brave enough to serve Christ anyway, Christ kindled a fire of love whose light and heat radiated through him and remains lit in the world to this very day.

You see, St. Paul teaches us to live as though it is not about us, anyway. Others may make fun of us when we do our best. They may say that we are selfish when we succeed, and worthless when we fail. Ignorant people may claim that we can't teach them anything, and wise people may call us fools. Our sources of pride may become the object of ridicule, and our dignity may be held in scorn. But St. Paul shows us his secret: we don't live for their opinions; we live for God. He could not live based on the opinions others had about him. He had to walk the narrow, higher path—he had to follow the same Christ who finished his life naked upon the Cross. And he did.

Accepting responsibilities means risking failure. Making friends opens us to the pain of betrayal. Rising to lead means standing to be judged. The very ones we love can cause us the greatest pain, but we can love them anyway. The fire of God's love is whipped into a bright heat by the winds of the fear of human rejection because Christian love is not fueled by the void of human approval. By faith, we can cling to a Savior who was crucified by a misguided world, and, on the cross with him, we can stretch out our arms to embrace the very ones who nail us there.

Pondering with Paul . . .

Key points

1. Leadership can reveal our weaknesses as much as it reveals our strengths. How am I handling this? Is Jesus trying to meet me there?
   A thought from St. Paul: 2 Corinthians 10:1-18

2. Leadership is about the bonds of trust we forge with those whom we influence as much as it is about vision and daring. Is there someone in my life with whom I need to spend more time connecting? What is my relationship like with those whom I am leading?
   Read Philippians 3:1-11

3. Leading in the footsteps of Christ calls us to not make everything about us. Where is Jesus summoning me to a deeper humility and abandonment of vain thoughts? Where is my vanity about human approval getting in the way of God's plan for my life?
   Read 1 Corinthians 4:8-13

Ten

Life on the Edge

And so, this is how it was to end. After denouncing the "dogs" who would undermine his followers in Philippi, the "wolves" who would attack his disciples in Ephesus, and after being rescued from the "lion's mouth," suffering the serpentine betrayal of his people in Jerusalem, and hearing the boorish scoffing of the members of the Areopagus, Paul the Apostle was shown the blade that would take his life in Rome. Little could he know then that the sword that would dispatch him from the suffering of this life to the reward laid up for him in heaven would one day be placed in his hand in millions of statues and icons that would bear his name. Little could he have foreseen when he described the word of God that he preached as "sharper than any two-edged sword, piercing to the division of soul and spirit, of joints and marrow" (Heb 4:12), that one day it would be a sword that would bring him to heaven even as it cut him down on earth.

Certainly, Paul had contemplated his death at length during the long years of his solitary imprisonment. But could he have ever imagined just how perfectly Jesus had arranged for his departure from this life? Even his death was a kind of poetic proclamation of the Word of God in symbols. He died as he had lived—courageously offering his life as a gift in the presence of dreadful threats. He died as he had lived—a man dying in peace for the salvation of a world intent on violence and

condemnation. He died as he had lived—on
the edge of a blade.[16]

*For the word of God is living and active, sharper than any two-
edged sword, piercing to the division of soul and of spirit, of
joints and marrow, and discerning the thoughts and intentions
of the heart.*

HEBREWS 4:12

Letting St. Paul coach us on our Christian journey
introduces us to a wild ride. Committing to the work
of Jesus Christ as he did, even though fully aware of our
weakness, moves us to the cutting edge of action. Maybe
that is why St. Paul refers to the Word of God as a "two-
edged sword, piercing to the division of soul and spirit"
(Heb 4:12). He felt the power of Christian Courage that
sees in every obstacle to love an opportunity for Christ's
power to flow through us. Surrender to Christ creates
lions out of lambs; the followers of Christ were meant to
lead the world.

The symbol of St. Paul is the two-edged sword.
Incredibly, it was the two-edged sword of the Word of
God that brought his soul to life and dispatched his body
to death. A sword is an amazing reality: two opposing
sides of metal, coming to a point on a cutting edge. It

16. Inspired by traditional accounts of Paul's martyrdom.

makes for a poignant symbol for the type of Christian leadership St. Paul embodied and coaches us through. Just like a Christian who meets the strength of Christ in the very place where they experience their own unique blend of human weakness, a sword has two sides, strong and flat, that are forever inseparable. And, like Christians whose courageous faith allows them to boast of their weaknesses, who lift up their heads before the intimidating fears that could otherwise dull the impact of their lives, the two sides of the sword come to an edge in a fine point. Christianity requires courage in the same way that a sword requires an edge. And a Christian soul is made to be used by Christ in the same way that a sword is wielded in the hand of a warrior—to set free a world bound by the effects of sin.

The inner act of courage that we show when we faithfully face the fears our weaknesses can cause within us is not the end of the story; it is just the beginning. On the other side of a life sharpened on the whetstone of our courageous faith is a blessing for the world that only God can give. This is because a Christian is never alone. A Christian heart rests in Jesus, and Jesus makes our hearts his home. He lives and acts through us. And so, our lives are never really about us anyway; if we allow Jesus to have his way with us, our lives can become the place of his blessing, and our love can bring with it the power of God's love. Indeed, it is a marvel to think that we are called to live as members of the Body of Christ. Is this not what St. Paul meant when he said that "it is no longer I who live, but Christ who lives in me" (Gal 2:20)?

How much more marvelous would it be if each and every baptized Christian lived from this power of Christ within! Even more marvelous if this were true in our individual lives. What would our world look like if we Christians decided to live our lives more on the edge of courage? What would our marriages look like if we overlooked the bruises and hurts of the past and braved the mercy of forgiveness? How would our friendships be transformed if we lived them in the pursuit of something greater than ourselves? How would our society be transformed if people decided to build new things in hope instead of destroy old things in fear? It would look . . . wonderful. But most of the time, hope just seems too good to be true. We don't brave the edge of life, because we are afraid that we will fall off!

Surely, St. Paul felt the same way at times. The Bible tells of three times, in particular, when St. Paul teetered on the knife-blade of the faith that he was called to walk. At each one of these times, when we see him at the edge of giving up, defeated and weary, Jesus comes to him to strengthen him in an exceptional way. St. Paul uses two particularly evocative phrases to describe these encounters: he writes that the Lord told him "I am with you" (Acts 18:10) and he says the Lord "stood by me" (2 Tm 4:17). In Greek, the words for "standing by"—even though slightly different (either *paristémi* or *ephistémi*)—share the same essential meaning as when the Lord says that he was "with" Paul (*meta sou*): Jesus revealed the strength of his presence to quicken Paul's courage to continue. Amazingly, the presence of Jesus does not remove the obstacle from St. Paul's path; instead, Jesus strengthens him, and tells him each time to persevere through what he is facing. The first time this happened was in Corinth, as he found his ministry utterly undermined by jealousy and was barred from preaching in the synagogue by his own Jewish people (see Acts 18:9-11). A second time, Jesus came as he sat enchained in a prison in Jaffa, far from any love and consolation on earth, and assured of only one thing—that the path he was on would lead him to death (see Acts 23:11). A third time, Jesus drew near him when he found himself literally abandoned by his friends and followers to face the angry judgment of a man with enough power to end Paul's life in a bloody death. As he sat in chains in Rome, Paul would recall the impact of that threat in poignant words as he left his spiritual legacy to St. Timothy: "At my first defense no one took my part; all deserted me. May it not be charged against them! But the Lord stood by me and gave me strength to proclaim the word fully" (2 Tm 4:16-17).

The Lord stood by me.

Christians are called to live life on the edge, but we do not live there alone. Jesus stood there long before us. This is what St. Paul meant when he talked about the wisdom of the Cross (see 1 Cor 1:18-25). And this is why, when he arrived in Corinth, he said that he "decided to know nothing among you except Jesus Christ and him crucified" (1 Cor 2:2). St. Paul knew that on the Cross, Jesus Christ confronted the full power of our sins and the full, awful, destructive power that our sins unleash in the lives of those we love. When Jesus hoisted the Cross to his shoulder, he felt the full burden of the depression, the lethargy, the negativity of those who remain pinned down by the fear of fatalism and futility. When he walked the path of the Cross, falling, being turned around and hassled on every side, he knew from the inside, experientially, the confusing power of the inner fog that keeps us from daring. As he was nailed to the Cross, he allowed the spikes to pin his hands and feet to the wood so that he could spiritually embrace all of those noble souls who are bound by fear into inaction. He chose to know the pain of a full three hours without being able to breathe, thirsty, in increasing pain under the noonday sun, to embody and enflesh the strife and toil of each one of us under our aching lifetimes battling with the fears that come when fatigue makes us count the cost. And he chose to go, alone, through the lonesome valley of death so that we who journey that dark way would never have to walk it alone.

Indeed, all souls who feel the fear of rejection and of wasted love can now know that another one—Jesus—stands with them in their solitude.

The Christian is never alone. Waiting on the other side of our fears, meeting our courage with his grace, is the presence of Jesus, and the gift that he wants to give the world through his disciples. If we are brave and choose to boast of our weaknesses—to "hold our heads high" like St. Paul—there is no limit to the impact God can give our actions on the world around us. Indeed, God wants to do great things—all things—through his body, the Church. He wants to raise the dead. He wants to spread the truth. He wants to inspire greatness in human hearts. He wants to heal broken spirits. He wants to restore and lift up. He wants to bring peace. He wants to do it all using the cutting edge of our faith-filled courage.

Which leaves us with the powerful choice to make: Will we dare to be free? When Our Lord stood before his apostles on the Sunday following his glorious Resurrection, he no sooner gave them peace than he sent them forth on a daring mission—to take his Gospel to the ends of the earth. His peace set their hearts free—free to hope, free to choose a path, free to innovate their culture, free to accomplish great things, free to lead the world back to him. Then, when he sent them forth, his sending summoned them to dare great things for him with that freedom. In the same way the freedom we receive from Christ brings with it a peace that will not leave us idle. Like Paul, surrendering to love is much more a beginning than an end. We must let his peace disturb ours. Daring to love Jesus means we will risk much, and labor hard, but it also means that we will be blessed by true love and rejoice deeply in God's dazzling beauty.

Indeed, Christians are the edge of the blade of God's work in the world, but in the end, those who dare to receive the freedom Christ wants to bestow do more than tread boldly across the world—they become friends of God, and saints. Like St. Paul, they are never alone. They know the love of Jesus. They dare great things for him, and, by daring, they lead their world.

For I am already on the point of being sacrificed;

the time of my departure has come.

I have fought the good fight,

I have finished the race,

I have kept the faith.

Henceforth there is laid up for me the crown of righteousness,

which the Lord, the righteous judge, will award to me on

that Day . . .

2 TIMOTHY 4:6-8